ROMAN CATHOLIC REVIVAL

Robert Abel

Valentine Publishing House
Denver, Colorado

Valentine Publishing House LLC
P.O. Box 27422, Denver, Colorado 80227.

Cover Graphics—Desert Isle Design LLC.

Library of Congress Control Number: 2007928690

Publisher's Cataloging-in-Publication Data

Abel, Robert.
      Roman Catholic Revival / Robert Abel.

        p. : ill. ; cm.

      ISBN–10: 0-9711536-8-X
      ISBN–13: 978-0-9711536-8-4
      Includes bibliographical references.

1. Catholic Church. 2. Church renewal—Catholic Church. 3. Spiritual life—
Catholic Church. 4. Spiritual warfare. I. Title.

BX1746 .A24 2007
282   2007928690

Printed in the United States of America.

TABLE OF CONTENTS

1205 A.D.
Prelude for Revival

It was a beautiful autumn sunrise, as the gentle breeze swept through the rolling hillside. Saint Francis found himself in a mystical display of glory, as brightly colored auburn and scarlet leaves fluttered through the brisk morning air. As he traveled north in the direction of Assisi, he noticed a decapitated stone church in a clearing through the thicket.

Turning aside from the path he had been following, he carefully trod through a lush meadow of wetland grass to investigate. Cautiously, he approached the heavy wooden doors that sealed the southern entrance. As he pressed against them, the weathered wood and rusty iron hinges began to groan with an ancient-sounding screech.

From inside the church, Francis could hear the sound of pigeons taking flight through the holes in the roof. Moving through the cobwebs that were stretched across the entrance of the door, he noticed a magnificent crucifix. Brilliant rays of sunlight were streaming through the holes in the roof and illuminating the Savior's redemptive work on the cross.

Kneeling down before the crucifix, Saint Francis began to pray, *"O great and glorious God, enlighten the darkness of my mind. Grant me enduring faith, certain hope, and perfect charity. Help me to embrace the depths of your love, that in all my ways, I may accomplish your good and perfect will."*

Looking up at the crucifix, Francis heard a voice calling out to him, *"Francis, rebuild my church. As you can see, it is falling down!"*

Immediately, Francis rose from the cold granite floor and went to work. He gathered his friends together and started repairing the breached walls of San Damiano chapel with stone and mortar. He worked hard all day cutting new roof timbers, repairing the stained glass windows, and expelling the wind and rain with new roof tiles.

During this time, Pope Innocent the third had a prophetic dream in which he witnessed the walls of the great Lateran Basilica, the symbol of the universal Church, slowly falling down. Before the utter collapse of the structure, a man wearing a simple habit, rushed to support the church to prevent its downfall.

After completing the repairs to San Damiano chapel, Francis and his band of brothers set out to Rome to ask the Supreme Pontiff's permission before founding a new religious order. Upon seeing Francis, Pope Innocent recognized him as the same man in his dream. He eagerly blessed Francis and his followers, knowing they would go forth to awaken a greatly needed revival.

After restoring two more chapels on the outskirts of Assisi, Francis soon realized that his calling to rebuild the Church far exceeded the task of reconstructing dilapidated buildings. He soon realized that God wanted him to reform the spiritual life of the Church, to strengthen the priesthood, to empower the laity—to ignite the fire for revival.

*Religion that is pure
and undefiled before God, the Father, is this:
to care for orphans and widows in their distress,
and to keep oneself unstained by the world.*

James 1:27

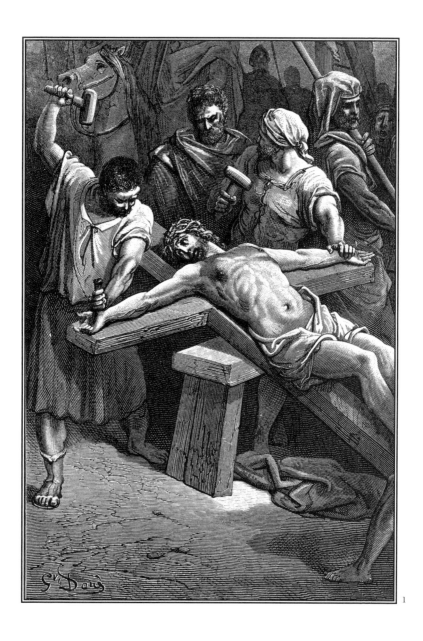

2

CHAPTER I

Since the Dawn of Creation
The Deadly Assault

War broke out in heaven; Michael and his angels fought against the dragon. The dragon and his angels fought back, but they were defeated, and there was no longer any place for them in heaven. The great dragon was thrown down, that ancient serpent, who is called the Devil and Satan, the deceiver of the whole world— he was thrown down to the earth, and his angels were thrown down with him.[2]

Since the dawn of creation a deadly presence of darkness has been on the rampage. After being stripped of his power and cast out of heaven, Satan devised a malicious plan. Calling forth his highest-ranking officials, he said, "Stop fighting amongst yourselves! Let's get even with God by harming his most treasured possession." Not long after, a spirit of deception entered the serpent and tempted Adam and Eve to commit the first sin.

After Adam and Eve disobeyed God by eating the forbidden fruit, their eyes were opened, and they acquired the knowledge of good and evil. Once the sinister presence of darkness entered their hearts, they could no longer interact with God the same as they had before. God being perfect light, holiness, and truth could no longer remain in the presence of his children after they had become defiled with evil.

Immediately after the fall, God devised a plan to win back the hearts of his beloved children. He made a decision to allow the devil to roam the earth because he wanted everybody to make a choice in their acceptance of his love and fellowship. He also wanted to test the hearts of his children to see which ones were true. Without the seductive presence of darkness roaming the earth, his children would be deprived of the ability to make a choice—would they choose a love affair with their Creator, or would they choose sin, sickness, and eternal separation?

Because God only wanted to develop authentic friendships with those who were truly interested in his goodness, he allowed Satan and the vast army of fallen angels to seduce as many humans as possible. If the devil could ensnare a soul with sin, he was allowed to take possession of that soul for all eternity. If God could establish a passionate love affair with anyone, he would allow that person to live in heavenly bliss for all eternity. There was only one rule—neither side could violate anyone's free will.

To make sure the devil would play fair, God stripped the angelic beings of their supernatural powers. The only thing the fallen angels could do is tempt the humans to sin, but once anyone committed a sin, the demons were allowed to access their lives. The more sinful agreements the humans made with the fallen angels, the more control the demons would acquire.

In the same way, God wanted to fill his children with the power of his Holy Spirit. From the very beginning, all God wanted was intimate fellowship with his beloved creation. When his beloved would cry out to be filled with his loving presence, they would be accepted, cleansed, and purified. When they wanted to serve the false gods of sinfulness, the demons were allowed to fill their hearts with a desire for more evil.

After the spiritual laws of the universe had been set in place, God immediately went to work with Cain and Abel. *In the course of time Cain brought to the Lord an offering of the fruit of the ground, and Abel for his part brought of the firstlings of his flock, their fat portions. And the Lord had regard for Abel and his offering, but for Cain and his offering he had no regard. So Cain was very angry, and his countenance fell.*[3]

The Lord tried to work with Cain by establishing a passionate love affair with his beloved son, but Cain's heart had become hardened. A deadly presence of darkness was pushing him to work harder and produce more wealth. He didn't want to give the best of his produce to the Lord. He had worked hard all day to acquire what he owned and had already made a decision to give his unwanted leftovers to the Lord.

God tried to explain the spiritual laws of the universe to Cain by saying, *"If you do well, will you not be accepted? And if you do not do well, sin is lurking at the door; its desire is for you, but you must master it."*[4] Unfortunately, the deadly presence of evil that was lurking at Cain's door was too strong. Soon a demonic force filled Cain's heart with evil intent. Evil spirits of anger and revenge manipulated his thoughts until the day *Cain rose up against his brother Abel, and killed him.*[5]

Meanwhile, the devil and his vast army of demons continued their assault against all of humanity. God tried to save as many souls as possible. He sent Moses to mediate a life-saving covenant. God wanted to establish a holy race, a royal priesthood, a people set apart. He wanted to be their God, and he wanted his beloved children to share in his heavenly inheritance.

As soon as Satan saw that God wanted to establish a holy nation, he divided his forces into two separate assault formations. One battalion of fallen angels was assigned to attack as worldly spirits, and the other group was assigned to attack as religious spirits. He sent the worldly spirits to assault the pagan nations, driving them to commit an ever-increasing amount of depravity. The other group of demons was sent against God's holy people with the intention of polluting the priesthood and distorting the true nature of worship.

When God called Moses to Mount Sinai and gave him the Ten Commandments, Satan listened very carefully to every word that God was saying: *"I am the Lord your God, who brought you out of the land of Egypt, out of the house of slavery; you shall have no other gods before me. You shall not make for yourself an idol, whether in the form of anything that is in heaven above, or that is on the earth beneath, or that is in the water under the earth. You shall not bow down to them or worship them; for I the Lord your God am a jealous God, punishing children for the iniquity of*

parents, to the third and the fourth generation of
those who reject me."⁶

After God's laws had been disclosed, Satan sent
the religious spirits into the Israelite camp to incite
the people to form a molten image. *When the people
saw that Moses delayed to come down from the mountain, the people gathered around Aaron, and said to
him, "Come, make gods for us, who shall go before us."⁷*
So Aaron gathered together all the gold jewelry from
the people, formed it into a mold, and cast an image
of a calf.

Afterward, the religious spirits continued their
assault on the pagan nations by persuading them to
fashion false gods for themselves. Whenever a man
carved a statue and started praying to it, a nearby
demon would accept the worship for himself. Every
so often the demons would grant the worshipers special favors to make their presence felt. That way the
worshipers would believe there were special powers
behind the images.

This practice became so prevalent that God had
to give strict laws to his people saying, *"When you
come into the land that the Lord your God is giving you,
you must not learn to imitate the abhorrent practices of
those nations. No one shall be found among you who
makes a son or daughter pass through fire, or who practices divination, or is a soothsayer, or an augur, or a sor-
cerer, or one who casts spells, or who consults ghosts or
spirits, or who seeks oracles from the dead. For whoever
does these things is abhorrent to the Lord; it is because
of such abhorrent practices that the Lord your God is
driving them out before you."⁸*

The pagan nations had become so polluted with the sin of idolatry, there was no other option but to have them destroyed. God didn't want to see the destruction of cities like Jericho, but the demonic activity was too strong. Satan had captured the hearts and souls of the entire town. They needed to be totally removed from the land, because they were a threat to the holy nation of Israel.

At first the Israelites were obedient to the Lord's instructions by driving out all the wicked inhabitants from the land, but after the first few battles, they started making agreements with nations like Gibeon. Instead of asking direction from the Lord, *Joshua made peace with them, guaranteeing their lives by a treaty; and the leaders of the congregation swore an oath to them.*[9] After the Israelites turned the nation of Gibeon into slaves, some of the Israelite men started falling in love with the Gibeon women. Not long after, the Gibeonites started introducing alternative forms of spirituality into the Israelite community.

Before long, *all the leading priests and the people also were exceedingly unfaithful, following all the abominations of the nations; and they polluted the house of the Lord that he had consecrated in Jerusalem. The Lord, the God of their ancestors, sent persistently to them by his messengers, because he had compassion on his people and on his dwelling place; but they kept mocking the messengers of God, despising his words, and scoffing at his prophets, until the wrath of the Lord against his people became so great that there was no remedy.*[10]

After the vast army of religious spirits had

successfully polluted the entire nation of Israel, God was forced to allow his children to fall into the hands of their enemies. Even though God's children spent nearly seventy years in captivity, the deadly assault didn't stop. The seductive spirits of religion continued to pervert the minds and hearts of the people to the point where the only remedy was for God to personally visit his creation.

In the fullness of time, God sent his only begotten Son into the world. Jesus left behind his divinity and took on the life of a carpenter. He came to earth to show us how to live, to teach us the way of love, and to pay the death penalty for our sins so that we could be reconciled with his heavenly Father.

As soon as Christ entered the world, Satan sent a division of demons to influence King Herod. When the wise men came to inquire about the newborn King of the Jews, Herod wanted to search for the child so that he could kill him. When the wise men did not return to share their findings, King Herod became enraged. Under the influence of demonic oppression, he ordered all the children in Bethlehem who were two years old and younger to be destroyed.

Joseph and Mary had already escaped with the Christ child to Egypt, but that didn't stop Satan. He continued looking for another opportunity and continued his assault the day the Lord entered the wilderness. He assumed that Jesus would be at his weakest point after fasting forty days, so he tempted him to turn rocks into loaves of bread. When that didn't work, he offered to give him all the riches of the world if he would bow down and worship him. Once Satan realized that Jesus was more powerful and could not be tempted, he quickly departed and sent a multitude of religious spirits to influence the Pharisees.

The system of religion that God had established had become so distorted that it was almost unrecognizable. The scribes and Pharisee's hearts had become so hardened, the Lord had to confront them by saying, *"You are from your father the devil, and you choose to do your father's desires. He was a murderer from the beginning and does not stand in the truth, because there is no truth in him. When he lies, he speaks according to his own nature, for he is a liar and the father of lies."*[11]

God wanted to establish a loving relationship with the scribes and Pharisees, but they were too busy practicing religion. Their lives were full of religious behaviors, yet they were opposed to the Spirit of God. Jesus tried to warn them by saying, *"Woe to you, scribes and Pharisees, hypocrites! For you lock people out of the kingdom of heaven. For you do not go in yourselves, and when others are going in, you stop them. Woe to you, scribes and Pharisees, hypocrites! For you cross sea and land to make a single convert, and you make the new convert twice as much a child of hell as yourselves."*[12]

If the religious leaders desired an authentic relationship with God, they would have been filled with God's Spirit, and they would have been able to impart that same Spirit to others. But unfortunately, a demonic spirit of religion had cut them off from

God. Instead of allowing themselves to be filled with God's love and allowing that love to flow into the lives of others, they were filled with a spirit of legalism that placed more importance on their external forms of worship.

Even though most of the religious leaders were living under the influence of demonic oppression, not all of them were opposed to God's Spirit. One of the scribes wanted to believe that the law of love was more important than the rules of religion. After listening to the wisdom of Jesus, he approached the Lord and asked, *"Which commandment is the first of all?"[13]*

Jesus answered, "The first is, 'Hear, O Israel: the Lord our God, the Lord is one; you shall love the Lord your God with all your heart, and with all your soul, and with all your mind, and with all your strength.' The second is this, 'You shall love your neighbor as yourself.' There is no other commandment greater than these."[14]

Then the scribe said to him, "You are right, Teacher; you have truly said that 'he is one, and besides him there is no other'; and 'to love him with all the heart, and with all the understanding, and with all the strength,' and 'to love one's neighbor as oneself,'—this is much more important than all whole burnt offerings and sacrifices."[15]

When Jesus saw that he answered wisely, he said to him, "You are not far from the kingdom of God."[16]

Unfortunately, most of the religious leaders didn't agree with God's law of love. The evil spirits had influenced their thoughts for so long that most believed the temple activities were all that was pleasing to God. Many of the religious leaders placed more importance on the rules and regulation of religion than on an authentic relationship with God. They were devoid of compassion and filled with a spirit of contempt toward anyone who didn't agree with their ideology. They went so far as to persecute others for the sake of their beliefs, like the time when Jesus entered the synagogue and noticed a man with a withered hand.

The scribe and Pharisees *watched him to see whether he would cure him on the sabbath, so that they might accuse him. And he said to the man who had the withered hand, "Come forward." Then he said to them, "Is it lawful to do good or to do harm on the sabbath, to save life or to kill?" But they were silent. He looked around at them with anger; he was grieved at their hardness of heart and said to the man, "Stretch out your hand." He stretched it out, and his hand was restored. The Pharisees went out and immediately conspired with the Herodians against him, how to destroy him.*[17]

Eventually the religious leaders killed the Son of God. They accused him of breaking the rules of their religion and handed him over to be crucified. A Roman soldier took a whip made out of straps of leather with sharpened pieces of bone attached and inflicted the full force of the whip across the Lord's body, tearing his flesh apart. After the soldiers forced him to carry a heavy cross to the place called Golgotha, they drove wrought iron spikes into his hands and feet, crucifying the Son of God on the cross of Calvary.

After the death of God's Son, the influence of religious spirits has continued to plague the Church throughout the centuries. Satan and his vast army of fallen angels have caused numerous holy wars, divisions, and conflicts over the papacy. Deadly spirits of religion have caused God's children to fight against one another and have instigated the most horrific persecutions imaginable during the Inquisitions, where both Protestants and witches were tortured and burned alive in the holy name of religion.

The deadly assault continues to this very day. Satan wants to establish his kingdom by polluting the minds and hearts of all who call themselves Christians. He wants to drive the presence of God out of his domain. Satan has a plan for thousands of people to die of starvation today, while millions more experience severe acts of violence, injustice, and depravity.

Satan's worldwide plan is to infiltrate the minds and hearts of those who work in the entertainment and news media. He wants to send forth a spirit of fear, causing the majority of the population to isolate themselves while growing more accustomed to watching random acts of violence, until his worldwide plan for destruction reaches epidemic proportions.

His plan also includes the infiltration of our schools. He has already assigned worldly spirits to the lives of teachers, college professors, administrative assistants, and political rights activists. He wants to rob young children of their innocence, teaching them about sexual acts and encouraging them to use birth control and experiment in homosexual behaviors.

He wants to infiltrate the minds and hearts of our government officials, causing them to legislate laws that are inherently evil. He wants to deprive the poor and needy, while the rich become more ensnared in materialistic bondage. Satan's plans also include a devious attack against the Catholic Church. The vast army of religious spirits that infiltrated the lives of the scribes and Pharisees are still at work today. The same tactics that the devil used when Peter issued the following warning are still in effect to this very hour:

False prophets also arose among the people, just as there will be false teachers among you, who will secretly bring in destructive opinions. They will even deny the Master who bought them—bringing swift destruction on themselves. Even so, many will follow their licentious ways, and because of these teachers the way of truth will be maligned. And in their greed they will exploit you with deceptive words. Their condemnation, pronounced against them long ago, has not been idle, and their destruction is not asleep.[18]

The vast army of religious spirits that Satan has sent against the Church will do everything in their power to keep people focused on the practice of religion, while preventing them from entering into an authentic relationship with the Blessed Trinity. These deadly spirits of religion want to cut God's children off from genuine fellowship. God wants to fill his children with his peace, power, and divine presence. The devil wants to pollute the spiritual atmosphere of the Church with a deadening spirit of stagnation.

Every time someone cries out to God in an attempt to establish a spirit-filled relationship, the religious spirits try to make that person feel unworthy. They want to block all spiritual unity with God by distorting his good and loving image. They want to fill the minds and hearts of believers with shame, self-condemnation, and the pride of religious superiority.

God wants to establish a loving relationship with all his children. The devil wants everyone to die in a state of complacency. God wants to fill all believers with his miracle-working power. The devil wants to contaminate the Church with a demonic spirit of stagnation.

Take a minute right now and ask yourself the following questions to see if you can pass the religious spirit test.

Can you authentically connect with the Spirit and presence of God within the first fifteen minutes of prayer? Yes ❏ No ❏

Do you know how to listen to the voice of the Good Shepherd? Yes ❏ No ❏

Can you hear clearly from God when it's time to make important decisions? Yes ❏ No ❏

After you receive direction and insight from the Lord, do you follow his instructions in complete obedience? Yes ❏ No ❏

Jesus has incredible plans for your life. He wants to establish a deeper and more passionate relationship with all his children. If there are any spirits of religion interfering with your ability to connect and commune with Christ, ask your heavenly Father to remove them. Invite the Holy Spirit into your heart right now. Allow yourself to be transformed by the person, power, and presence of the Lord Jesus Christ.

*Then Jesus said to the crowds and to his disciples,
"The scribes and the Pharisees sit on Moses' seat;
therefore, do whatever they teach you and
follow it; but do not do as they do, for they
do not practice what they teach."*

Matthew 23:1–3

CHAPTER II

Call No One on Earth Your Father
Restoring Our Image of God

They do all their deeds to be seen by others; for they make their phylacteries broad and their fringes long. They love to have the place of honor at banquets and the best seats in the synagogues, and to be greeted with respect in the marketplaces, and to have people call them rabbi. But you are not to be called rabbi, for you have one teacher, and you are all students. And call no one your father on earth, for you have one Father— the one in heaven.[2]

After the Roman emperor Augustus Caesar took control of the Jewish nation, he appointed a system of governors to rule over the territory. These governors appointed procurators and tetrarchs over different providences, along with tax collectors who extracted exorbitant fees from the Israelites. In an attempt to maintain the peace, the chief priest, elders, and scribes made agreements with the Roman officials so that they could preserve their ceremonial laws and continue practicing the temple purification rituals.

After these agreements were made, political corruption entered the priesthood. The high priests and religious leaders were supposed to be obedient to God. The Lord wanted to fill them with his Holy Spirit, so that they could speak on his behalf, and draw the hearts of the people back toward their heavenly Father. Instead of being obedient servants of God, they ended up selling their obedience to a system of religious behaviors tainted with corrupt political agendas.

During this time, the scribes had been making their living by writing, copying, and translating the law. They loved dressing up in long robes, taking the most important seats in the synagogue, and being honored with terms of respect in the marketplace. In an attempt to safeguard the sanctity of the law, the scribes had developed a complex system of teaching the law that took a great amount of time and resources to master. Over the years they had been adding additional requirements to the law that took the focus off God, and put it on their own examples and behaviors.

The Pharisees also loved dressing up in long robes and receiving the terms of respect from others. The Pharisees tried to be living examples of the law. The scribes would interpret the law, and the Pharisees would demonstrate how the law was to be lived out. At one point the Pharisees thought they had become so holy that they needed to separate themselves from the people. They didn't want to associate with anything impure, contaminated, or unclean. They ended up spending the majority of their time focusing on ceremonial purity, washing cups and dishes, and keeping the smallest details of the law, like tithing on mint and dill.

Before long the entire system of worship had become polluted with corruption. The scribes, Pharisees, and chief priests had become ensnared in the trap of clericalism. Instead of being obedient to God's Spirit, they had set up a system of rules and regulations to control the people and use them for financial gain. Unfortunately, the same characteristics that hindered the holy priesthood two thousand years ago are still in effect today.

It was for this reason that Jesus said, *"Call no one your father on earth, for you have one Father—the one in heaven. Nor are you to be called instructors, for you have one instructor, the Messiah. The greatest among you will be your servant. All who exalt themselves will be humbled, and all who humble themselves will be exalted."[3]*

Jesus gave us this command because he doesn't want us to make our religious leaders, or a system of religious behaviors, more important than our relationship with our heavenly Father. A priest is supposed to be filled with God's Spirit so that he can speak on God's behalf. It is the priest's job to lead others to God, not to acquire a congregation of people whose sole purpose is to watch him perform religious behaviors for an hour on Sunday morning.

Jesus didn't come to establish a system of religious behaviors; he came so that men could be reconciled to his Father in heaven. This is the entire reason why Jesus shed his blood on the cross at Calvary—so that we could enter into an authentic relationship with the Blessed Trinity. The job of a good priest is to connect men with God. When a new convert wants to know more about God, it is the priest's job to show him how to have his sin's forgiven, how to be filled with the Holy Spirit, and how to live a life that is pleasing to the Father.

A good example of a devout servant comes from the life of Saint Paul. After his conversion experience, he called himself a spiritual father. In 1 Corinthians 4:15–16 he needed to correct the Church in Corinth like a little child so he said, *"For though you might have ten thousand guardians in Christ, you do not have many fathers. Indeed, in Christ Jesus I became your father through the gospel. I appeal to you, then, be imitators of me."*

Paul was a true spiritual father to the church in Corinth. He actually laid down his life in service, toil, and many hardships to raise spiritual children unto the Lord Jesus. In no way did Paul want to set himself up as a high priest, so that he could parade around in a long robe, take the most important seat at synagogue, and try to gain control over the temple treasury, so that everybody would worship him in place of God.

There's a difference between setting yourself up in place of God and helping other people reach out and connect with the real God. This is the point Jesus was making when he said, *"You have one Father—the one in heaven... You have one instructor, the Messiah."* It is extremely important for everybody's salvation to reach out and enter into an authentic relationship with their heavenly Father. The Lord doesn't want anyone to give the sacred place of worship within their hearts to a mere man, especially when that man doesn't have the power to save souls from death.

When I was growing up, I was taught to respect the clergy because the priest represented God, and in some cases, took the place of Christ. For example, when the priest consecrates the bread and wine, he is acting in the place of Christ. I believe many Catholics have heard the same teaching as defined in the Catechism: *It is the same priest, Christ Jesus, whose sacred person his ministers truly represents. Now the minister, by reason of the sacerdotal consecration which he has received, is truly made like to the high priest and possesses the authority to act in the power and place of the person of Christ himself (virtute ac persona ipsius Christi).*[4]

This is a profound truth of the Catholic Church. The only problem with focusing on a single element of the truth is that the bigger picture can become distorted. In my situation, I was taught this truth at a very early age. I believed the priest took the place of Christ. At one point in my walk, the Church actually became my God. I thought that if I did everything the Church told me to do that I would be in right relationship with God.

I lived in this shallow form of spirituality for many years, until the day I had an actual encounter with God. At that point my spiritual eyes were opened, and I realized that I had been making the Catholic Church a false god. I was kneeling in church praying one day, when the God of the universe made his presence very real to me. It was then that I realized God was different than the Catholic Church. That God is actually bigger and more powerful than the Catholic Church. God existed before the beginning of time, and when the Church comes to an end, God will still exist.

It was an eye-opening experience to realize and acknowledge that the Church was no longer my God. That it is the Church's responsibility to connect me with the real God, not to become a false god unto me. The same is true with the parish priest. The role of a true spiritual father is to connect his spiritual children to God Himself—not to take the place of God in their lives.

Looking back at my situation, I realize I was only given half the story. According to the Catechism, *The whole People of God participates in these three offices of Christ and bears the responsibilities for mission and service that flow from them.*[5] *The laity are made to share in the priestly, prophetical, and kingly office of Christ; they have therefore, in the Church and in the world, their own assignment in the mission of the whole People of God.*[6]

In other words the Catechism is saying: *The Christian faithful are those who, inasmuch as they have been incorporated in Christ through Baptism, have been constituted as the people of God; for this reason, since they have become sharers in Christ's priestly, prophetic, and royal office in their own manner, they are called to exercise the mission which God has entrusted to the Church to fulfill in the world, in accord with the condition proper to each one.*[7]

A good example of how the Christian faithful are called to carry out their priestly, prophetic, and royal office of Christ comes from my work with the homeless. While working on the streets of Denver, I have many times encountered men who have never received Baptism. According to the Catechism in section 1257, Baptism is necessary for salvation.

If I come across an emergency situation where a homeless man is dying in a back alley late at night, the Catechism in section 1256 says, *In case of necessity, anyone, even a non-baptized person, with the required intention, can baptize, by using the Trinitarian baptismal formula.*[8]

If after I share the love of Christ with a dying man, and he wants to have his sins forgiven, I can ask him to make a profession of faith and baptize him in the name of the Father, Son, and Holy Spirit. According to the Catechism, *By baptism all sins are forgiven, original sin and all personal sins, as well as all punishment for sin.*[9] Once the man's sins are removed, he can pass from this world to the next, knowing that he has been restored to God's fellowship, through the ministry of reconciliation.

By baptizing the homeless man, I would be fulfilling my priestly, prophetic, and royal office in Christ. I would also be acting in obedience to the Lord's command when he said, *"All authority in heaven and on earth has been given to me. Go therefore and make disciples of all nations, baptizing them in the name of the Father and of the Son and of the Holy Spirit, and teaching them to obey everything that I have commanded you."*[10]

In this sense, the laity and the clergy are both coworkers in Christ. We should be working together on the same team, fulfilling the same mission and purpose in life. All members of the Church need to acknowledge that we have one Lord and Master, Jesus Christ, and that we all need to seek a deeper fellowship with him on a daily basis. Christ is the head of the Church, and both the clergy and laity need to surrender their lives into his service. One party is not any better than any other. According to the Word of God, the body of Christ has many different members, and even though we are called differently, we are all one body:

> *For just as the body is one and has many members, and all the members of the body, though many, are one body, so it is with Christ. Indeed, the body does not consist of one member but of many. If the whole body were an eye, where would the hearing be? If the whole body were hearing, where would the sense of smell be?*[11]

> *But as it is, God arranged the members in the body, each one of them, as he chose. If all were a single member, where would the body be? As it is, there are many members, yet one body. The eye cannot say to the hand, "I have no need of you," nor again the head to the feet, "I have no need of you."*[12]

> *On the contrary, the members of the body that seem to be weaker are indispensable, and those members of the body that we think less honorable we clothe with greater honor, and our less respectable members are treated with greater respect; whereas our more respectable members do not need this. But God has so arranged the body, giving the greater honor to the inferior member, that there may be no dissension within the body, but the members may have the same care for one*

another. Now you are the body of Christ and individually members of it.[13]

All members of Christ's body are of equal importance, and all have been given their own assignments and responsibilities that need to be accomplished in this lifetime. It is for this reason that all members of Christ's body need to work together in unity. There should be no difference between the clergy and the laity; both are extremely valuable members of Christ's body, and both need to work together to advance God's kingdom here on earth.

Unfortunately, in the Church there seems to be a lie that says, *Christ is way too holy to get involved with the everyday affairs of the laity.* The laity have been assigned priestly, prophetic, and royal responsibilities, but many of them have been conditioned to merely sit in the pew for an hour on Sunday. Many parishioners feel totally unworthy to perform any kind of ministry. This lie says, *only priests and deacons can perform ministry*, hence the clergy is overworked and the laity are deteriorating in a state of spiritual stagnation.

Another misconception I learned during my childhood was that the Pope took the place of Christ. The Catechism says, *For the Roman Pontiff, by reason of his office as Vicar of Christ, and as pastor of the entire Church has full, supreme, and universal power over the whole Church, a power which he can always exercise unhindered.*[14] The word *Vicar* means *one who stands in for or acts for another.* In other words, the Pope is a *representative* of Christ and an *ambassador* for Christ. In the same way, all Christians are called to be *ambassadors* for Christ.

According to Sacred Scripture, *if anyone is in Christ, there is a new creation: everything old has passed away; see, everything has become new! All this is from God, who reconciled us to himself through Christ, and has given us the ministry of reconciliation; that is, in Christ God was reconciling the world to himself, not counting their trespasses against them, and entrusting the message of reconciliation to us. So we are ambassadors for Christ, since God is making his appeal through us; we entreat you on behalf of Christ, be reconciled to God.*[15]

When we look more closely at the Word of God, it says *if anyone is in Christ*, meaning all members of the body who consider themselves to be Christian, are called into the ministry of reconciliation as ambassadors for Christ. The word *ambassador* means *representative*. An ambassador is commissioned to speak on behalf of his home country. In the same way, all Christians are called to be ambassadors for Christ. We are called to represent the heavenly kingdom of Christ here on earth.

When Christ gave us the great commission, he assigned all believers the responsibility to go forth and make disciples of all nations. To accomplish this, we are called to walk the walk just like Jesus did. We are called to teach what Christ taught and do what Christ did. Jesus is our model. We are his anointed agents. We are called into a sinful world to share God's love with others. We are called to tell people how they can have their sins forgiven. We are called to minister reconciliation to those who are not in right relationship with God. We are called to restore men to their heavenly Father.

Another reason why the Lord doesn't want us calling any man on earth our father is because he doesn't want us to project our human relationship dynamics on the Deity. Many times our earthly fathers and parish priests fall short. It is possible for them to be deceived, grow complacent in their faith, or become defiled with impure intentions. By projecting the shortcomings of our earthly parents on God, we damage our ability to love, trust, and enter into a meaningful relationship with our heavenly Father.

Many times these subconscious drives are so subtle that we don't even know they are occurring. For example, when I was a little boy, my brother and sisters and I would sit two feet away from the television and watch cartoons all afternoon. When my father came home from work, he would walk past the television and enforce the house rules.

The television set we were watching was the old tube-type. We would be hanging on every word, then all of a sudden my dad would walk past and turn the television off, because we were either sitting too close or because we had the volume up too high. Once the set was turned off, it took several minutes to warm back up and regain the picture.

In these early encounters with my father, I was being subconsciously programmed in the ways that I would view the world, authority figures, and to some degree my heavenly Father. When I was a little boy, my parents were my first representatives of God. I looked to them for my very existence and survival. Without their life-giving care, I would have died of neglect. As a little boy, I viewed my parents as all-knowing, all-powerful caregivers.

When my father came home from work, he represented a distant authority figure who would enforce the house rules with a quick zap of the stitch. The laws for the television were simple; sit six feet away with the sound so low it was almost impossible to hear anything. If the laws were broken, my all-powerful lawgiver would inflict the proper punishment.

Deep in my subconscious, I learned at an early age that this is how the world works. Without a real encounter with God, my earliest source of information from my earthly father would be subconsciously projected upon my heavenly Father. If my earthly father was a cold, distant, authority figure whose only purpose was to punish the disobedient rule breakers, that's how I would have grown up, projecting the same views on God.

The first step in healing our image of God comes by replacing the distorted images with the truth. If you want to know who God the Father is, all you have to do is look at the life of Christ. When Phillip said, *"Lord, show us the Father, and we will be satisfied." Jesus said to him, "Have I been with you all this time, Philip, and you still do not know me? Whoever has seen me has seen the Father. How can you say, 'Show us the Father'? Do you not believe that I am in the Father and the Father is in me?"*[16]

If we want to know who God the Father is, all

we have to do is look at the life of Christ. We can see the Father's compassion for the hungry when Jesus fed the multitude. We can see the Father's mercy when Jesus forgave the woman who had been caught in adultery. We can see the Father's love when Jesus restored the sight to the blind, cleansed the leper, and empowered the lame to rise up and walk.

The very nature and character of our heavenly Father is love. God sent his only begotten son into the world to show us his love. He wants to establish a passionate relationship with all his beloved children. He wants to remove our distorted images and replace them with his truth. He wants to heal all our wounds. He wants to fill us with his Holy Spirit. He wants to live a life of communion with us through his intimate fellowship.

I first started developing a more intimate relationship with my heavenly Father the day a friend of mine told me about the books he was reading. He was researching the lives of the modern-day Saints, great men of God who were conducting healing services so powerful that people would rise from their wheelchairs and start walking. He noticed a common thread in their lives—they all had a close relationship with their heavenly Father.

After hearing about this, I set out to develop a closer relationship with my Abba Father. I started praying at a small table with four chairs. After taking a seat in one of the chairs, I invited the three persons of the Trinity to join me. At first is seemed difficult and awkward, but after a while I began speaking to my Abba Father from my heart. I realized that I had spent most of my life distant from his fellowship. I believed information about God the Father, but I never took the time to really get to know him.

My prayer time really grew exciting when I started meditating on God's Word in the presence of the Trinity. I would read passages like the one where Jesus said, *"As you, Father, are in me and I am in you, may they also be in us, so that the world may believe that you have sent me. The glory that you have given me I have given them, so that they may be one, as we are one, I in them and you in me, that they may become completely one, so that the world may know that you have sent me and have loved them even as you have loved me."[17]*

After reading these kinds of Scripture passages, I would have the most incredible conversations with the three Persons of the Trinity. I pictured the Lord Jesus sitting at the table looking at me with the most beautiful eyes. My Abba Father would sit directly across from me filled with a warm and gentle Spirit. At times all I could do was repeat his name over and over again, asking him to take care of me in the same way a three-year-old boy would cry out to his earthly father.

There's nothing to fear. The Blessed Trinity has incredible plans for your life. Why not take a moment right now and invite the Blessed Trinity to join you in prayer? Start by finding a quiet place in your home and come humbly before the Lord your God. If you have been living a life devoid of God's intimate fellowship, ask your heavenly Father's forgiveness. Speak to the Blessed Trinity from your heart. Tell all three

Persons of the Trinity you are sorry for exchanging the glory of the immortal God for any other types of false gods.

If you have been making the parish priest your god, ask the Lord for his forgiveness. If you have been turning the Catholic Church into a false god, ask your heavenly Father to set you free from all forms of spiritual bondage. There's only room in your heart for one God. Jesus wants to come into your heart right now. He wants to cleanse and purify your life with the power of his Holy Spirit.

If you have been projecting unhealthy images on God based on the actions of your earthly father, or from your parish priest, take a minute right now and ask the Lord's forgiveness. If there's anyone that you need to forgive, say the words out loud. I forgive my earthly father for yelling, hurting, abandoning, threatening, and not caring about me... I forgive my parish priest for... Release the people who hurt you and surrender everything into the Lord's loving hands.

Take a minute right now to thank your heavenly Father for calling you out of the darkness and into the light. You are a child of the King. You are an ambassador for Christ. You have been assigned the responsibility of priest, prophet, and king. You have been commissioned to go forth and make disciples of all nations.

That evening they brought to him
many who were possessed with demons;
and he cast out the spirits with a word,
and cured all who were sick.
This was to fulfill what had been
spoken through the prophet Isaiah,
"He took our infirmities and bore our diseases."

Matthew 8:16–17

CHAPTER III

The Growing Trend of Suffering Taking Authority over Evil

Then they brought to him a demoniac who was blind and mute; and he cured him, so that the one who had been mute could speak and see. But when the Pharisees heard it, they said, "It is only by Beelzebul, the ruler of the demons, that this fellow casts out the demons."[2]

Jesus tried to explain the deeper realities of the spirit realm to the religious leaders, but their minds were darkened and their hearts were hardened. They refused to acknowledge the deeper truths of God and continued arguing with the Lord, so he rebuked them by saying, *"You brood of Vipers! How can you speak good things, when you are evil? For out of the abundance of the heart the mouth speaks. The good person brings good things out of a good treasure, and the evil person brings evil things out of an evil treasure. I tell you, on the day of judgment you will have to give an account for every careless word you utter."[3]*

Unfortunately, the same amount of fear, lack of faith, and negativity that was present in the lives of the Pharisees, has continued to affect the Church until this very day. For example, what is easier to say to the man with cancer—sickness is your cross to bear, or be healed in the name of Jesus? If the clergy has the authority to act in the person of Christ, then why don't more parish priests start healing people like Jesus did? Why would anyone want to preach a sermon on suffering when they could be talking about the healing power of Jesus?

Instead of moving with the power and authority of Christ, many priests have been spending the majority of their time working as office administrators. In fact, there's a growing number of priests and leading theologians who don't even believe in the devil's existence. The roaring lion that prowls around looking for the ruin of souls has been reduced down to a metaphor, or an abstract way to describe the language used in the Bible.

Whenever a Gospel reading about the devil or demons comes across the Church's lectionary, many priests bypass the subject completely. Others may acknowledge the devil's existence, but they don't want to talk about anything negative or offend anyone in the congregation. These types of behaviors, along with the failure to acknowledge a proper biblical worldview, continue to cause numerous problems in a variety of ways.

First of all, without the acknowledgment of the devil's existence, the Gospel message doesn't make sense. Without a belief in the devil, many people start to question why an all-powerful and loving God would allow his Son to be crucified. *Does God take pleasure in suffering? If God is so sick to crucify his own Son, how should we expect to be treated?* Maybe this type of reasoning helps explain the growing number of sermons that are being preached on the need to suffer.

Without a belief in the devil's existence, the present state of our world makes God look bad. The devil is the main instigator of sin, sickness, suffering, and disease. When we fail to believe in the devil's existence, then we have no choice but to blame the works of the devil on God. By denying the devil's existence, the only other logical conclusion is that God must like sin, sickness, and disease, because there sure is a lot of it going on in our world today.

The most damaging consequences come when we fail to use our authority in Christ. By denying the devil's existence, we are also denying a need to protect ourselves from the devil's schemes and devices. By failing to believe in demonic illness, we have forfeited our rights to take authority over the devil's works, and by doing so, have failed to administer the healing power of Jesus. A good example of this comes from the Gospel of Luke:

There appeared a woman with a spirit that had crippled her for eighteen years. She was bent over and was quite unable to stand up straight. When Jesus saw her, he called her over and said, "Woman, you are set free from your ailment." When he laid his hands on her, immediately she stood up straight and began praising God.[4]

Afterward the Pharisees started attacking Jesus for healing on the sabbath. He responded to them by saying, *"You hypocrites! Does not each of you on the sabbath untie his ox or his donkey from the manger, and lead it away to give it water? And ought not this woman, a daughter of Abraham whom Satan bound for eighteen long years, be set free from this bondage on the sabbath day?"⁵*

When we take a closer look at the Word of God, we see Jesus interacting with the people, moving among them, teaching, and healing those who were sick. He's not hiding behind a cleric's outfit or locked away in a parish office somewhere. The woman in this passage didn't need an appointment set two weeks in advance to see the Lord. She didn't even need to ask for help. Jesus was the one who noticed that she needed healing, and because of his great love and compassion, he called her over.

We also see her physical ailment being caused by a demonic spirit. An evil spirit entered her body and crippled her for eighteen years. Because Jesus has authority over all the works of the devil, he gave a simple command. After Jesus laid his hands on her, the demonic spirit fled her presence, and the woman regained her strength.

Notice we do not see Jesus taking the opportunity to talk about the redemptive value of suffering in this situation. He does not try to convince anyone that demonic oppression is pleasing to God. He doesn't even mention that being crippled was her cross to bear. God is a God of love, power, and healing—not a God of sickness, disease, and suffering!

Before we look at this problem more closely, let's first establish that the Bible is the Word of God. The Catechism says, *God is the author of Sacred Scripture. "The divinely revealed realities, which are contained and presented in the text of Sacred Scripture, have been written down under the inspiration of the*

Holy Spirit."[6] Because *God is Truth itself, whose words cannot deceive,*[7] we can rest assured that according to the Catechism, *The Sacred Scriptures contain the Word of God and, because they are inspired, they are truly the Word of God.*[8]

When the Bible says that Satan is a real, live fallen angel who was kicked out of heaven with a third of the heavenly host and cast down to earth, you can rest assured that every word is true. When Sacred Scripture says that *Satan went out from the presence of the Lord, and inflicted loathsome sores on Job from the sole of his foot to the crown of his head,*[9] you should also believe the devil has the power to cause demonic illness.

Sacred Scripture and the Catechism both speak about the devil's existence, but before a person can actually believe in the devil, he or she needs to have an encounter with evil. This encounter works the same way as any other spiritual encounter. Once we experience something supernatural that cannot be explained with our intellect, then our "head knowledge" becomes a genuine belief.

If you have ever met a man who claims to be an atheist, you know that he has never had an encounter with God. The man may have read many books about God, or listened to other people's testimonies, but all the information is speculative head knowledge. Once the man has an encounter with God, his spiritual eyes will be opened and he will acquire the ability to believe in God's existence.

The same is true with the devil. Before anyone

will be able to believe in the devil's existence, that person will need to have an actual encounter with the presence of darkness. Once they do, their spiritual eyes will be opened—their theological opinions will be transformed into an actual belief.

A good modern-day example of the devil's existence that most people can relate to comes from road rage. Let's say a very nice man is in a hurry. He's late to a church meeting, when all of a sudden another motorist cuts him off. If he slams on his brakes and spills his coffee, the spirit of anger that comes over him is not coming from the Holy Spirit.

If the man makes agreements with the demonic spirit of anger, he may hit the accelerator, cut the other motorist off, make obscene hand gestures, and utter profanities. He also has the option to invoke the power and authority of Jesus. If in the heat of the attack the man were to call upon the Lord, and suddenly the evil spirit of rage departed, leaving behind a spirit of peace, the man's spiritual eyes would be opened. He would experience a minor form of deliverance. His encounter with evil would be offset with an infilling of the Holy Spirit.

Hopefully, a belief in the devil's existence would never scare any of God's children, because according to Sacred Scripture, *God did not give us a spirit of cowardice but rather of power and love and self-control.*[10] Fear is one of the main tactics the devil uses to go unhindered in his assault against humanity. Saint Ambrose says, *"One who entrusts himself to God does not dread the devil. If God is for us, who is against us?"*[11]

When it comes to the devil, there's nothing to fear. Satan has already been defeated. Jesus has given power over all the works of the devil to his disciples. If you are wondering if you are one of the Lord's disciples, the Catechism says, *In all of his life Jesus presents himself as our model. He is "the perfect man," who invites us to become his disciples and follow him.*[12] Anyone who accepts the Lord's teaching and dedicates his life to follow Christ in obedience, should consider himself to be a disciple.

In the Gospel of Luke, Jesus gave his disciples power over all the works of the enemy. *Jesus called the twelve together and gave them power and authority over all demons and to cure diseases, and he sent them out to proclaim the kingdom of God and to heal.*[13] In this situation, the power and authority given to the twelve disciples could be compared to the power given to the priesthood. Through the laying on of hands at their ordination, every priest receives the power to drive out demons, cure the sick, and to preach the Good News.

We also see in the Gospel of Luke that Jesus sent forth seventy more disciples with the same mission. When this group returned from their first missionary assignment, they said with great joy, *"Lord, in your name even the demons submit to us!" He said to them, "I watched Satan fall from heaven like a flash of lightning. See, I have given you authority to tread on snakes and scorpions, and over all the power of the enemy; and nothing will hurt you."*[14]

The power over evil has already been given to all disciples. It was first given to the priesthood when the twelve were sent forth, and then it was given to the laity when the seventy were sent forth. This power comes from the Holy Spirit, which is imparted at every believer's Baptism and Confirmation.

Once the Holy Spirit dwells within the heart of a disciple, all you need to do is start putting that power into action. When the demonic attack of road rage comes upon you, all you need to do is invoke the name of Jesus. Once you learn how to take authority over your own thoughts and behaviors, the Holy Spirit will show you how to use the same principles to drive evil out of your home, environment, and workplace. God wants all of his children to move with his power and authority. It has been given to every baptized and confirmed parishioner; all we need to do is start using it.

Another problem that occurs within society when the Church fails to use its authority over evil comes from a story about a drunk driver. One day a man named Bill was tempted by evil to get drunk in an attempt to escape his problems. When Bill was driving home, he lost control of his car and crashed into the side of a minivan.

Two young children inside the van died, and the mother was paralyzed. Clearly this is the result of sin and the work of the devil. It is not God's desire for Bill to get drunk and violate the laws of society. It is not God's desire for the mother to lose her children and to spend the rest of her life in a wheelchair. Although, when events like these happen, most people ignore the devil's involvement and spend the rest of their lives being angry with God.

I'm sure there are thousands of accidents every day that our heavenly Father would like to prevent, but God doesn't violate anyone's free will. When the Church denies the existence of evil and fails to take an active stand against Satan's devices, then the devil gains more power and influence over our world.

A good example of this is described in the book of Daniel when an angelic messenger was sent by God to help Daniel. Because of the great spiritual battle that ensued over the city, the prince of Persia was able to oppose the messenger for twenty-one days. Finally Michael the Archangel was called into battle, and afterward the messenger described the situation to Daniel as follows:

Do not fear, Daniel, for from the first day that you set your mind to gain understanding and to humble yourself before your God, your words have been heard, and I have come because of your words. But the prince of the kingdom of Persia opposed me twenty-one days. So Michael, one of the chief princes, came to help me, and I left him there with the prince of the kingdom of Persia.[15]

Many times God sends his Holy Spirit and his angelic messengers to warn us of upcoming dangers, but because of the spiritual battle that is ensuing all around us, we fail to recognize his softly spoken voice. When this happens, the devil is allowed to continue his deadly assault against all of humanity.

Another serious problem that is caused by the lack of belief in the devil's existence is the growing amount of theology on suffering. When the Church turns its back on the devil's existence, there is no one else to blame for human suffering except God. Many times when someone is diagnosed with an incurable disease, parishioners are quick to point out, *Illness must be your cross to bear.*

The cross is an instrument of death. Christians are required to put their fleshly desires to death. In order to become a disciple of Christ, we need to surrender our self-willed ways to the Lord and start walking in obedience. We need to put to death anything that hinders our ability to serve God in spirit and in truth, to put to death anything that keeps us from fully following Jesus, anything that keeps us from proclaiming the Gospel message, anything that keeps us from loving and serving the Lord with all of our strength.

Under this definition, sickness and disease can never be considered a cross to bear. Cancer and any other form of demonic illness only hinders our service to the Lord. It robs us of our strength, finances, and joy. The Bible describes sickness as a curse, a result of disobedience. It is usually defined as punishment for sin.

God does not inflict sickness on anybody. He simply removes his protection from us when we do sin. God is pure light, holiness, and truth. When we sin, he is forced to remove his presence from us, and afterward we are left vulnerable to attack. Once this happens, the devil has the right to enter our lives and punish us through the open doorway of our own sinful behaviors.

Another example of how evil can come upon us through an unhealthy desire to suffer comes from a story about two men who started fasting. One man gave up food in an attempt to draw closer to God. He converted all his food hunger into God hunger. When he cried out to the Lord with all his strength, the Lord ministered to him in life-changing ways, filling his body with the power of the Holy Spirit. By fasting with the proper intentions, the man's mind was renewed, his emotions were healed, and his body was supported through the Lord's Spirit.

The other man started fasting with the intention to suffer. He wanted to punish himself to save poor souls from purgatory. Even though fasting is a godly principle, because the man was fasting with the intention to suffer and inflict punishment upon himself, the devil had the right to enter his body and help him fulfill his desires. Eventually this man developed stomach ulcers.

One man fasted for the Lord because he wanted to grow closer to Christ. The other man fasted to suffer because he thought that suffering was pleasing to God. The man who was hungry for God was filled with God's Spirit. The man who wanted to suffer gave the devil a right to attack his body.

God takes no pleasure in human suffering. He only wants our love and obedience. Suffering is almost always a calling for a deeper relationship with the Lord. It is a calling for holiness, a time to grow, a time to make changes, a time to learn lessons, a time to deepen our faith and pursue God like never before. Any type of hardship that we encounter in life is always a calling for more holiness and a deeper conversion experience.

Almost every time suffering is mentioned in the Bible, it is associated with the struggle necessary to advance God's kingdom here on earth. For example, when Paul was locked away in prison for proclaiming the Gospel message, he wrote to Timothy saying, *"Do not be ashamed, then, of the testimony about our Lord or of me his prisoner, but join with me in suffering for the gospel, relying on the power of God."*[16]

There's a difference in suffering for the sake of the Gospel and suffering the results of demonic oppression and illness. It was very dangerous to be a missionary during the first century. It still is in many parts of the world. Christians are still being persecuted, tortured, and locked away in prison for spreading the Gospel message in many parts of the Middle East.

In this passage, Paul is encouraging Timothy to fight the good fight of faith. He is saying, go forth with all boldness. Spread the Gospel message. Don't be ashamed of the Lord. Join with me in proclaiming the Gospel message, and if suffering and persecution come your way, rejoice, for great will your reward be in heaven.

Another example describing the proper context for Christian suffering comes from the book of Peter when he said, *"Keep your conscious clear, so that, when you are maligned, those who abuse you for your good conduct in Christ may be put to shame. For it is better to suffer for doing good, if suffering should be God's will, than to suffer for doing evil."*[17]

In this passage Peter points out two different types of suffering—one kind comes from preaching the Gospel message and living a holy life in an ungodly world, the other type comes from the results of sinful behaviors. When we sin by breaking the natural, spiritual, or man-made laws of the universe, we can expect to pay the appropriate consequences, usually in the form of suffering.

God desires holiness and obedience. When you find yourself in a place of suffering, instead of thinking that God wants you to suffer, turn to your heavenly Father and allow yourself to meet God in the midst of your pain. Use the painful circumstances to motivate you into a deeper relationship with Christ.

If your suffering is caused by your own sinfulness, ask the Lord's forgiveness. If your suffering is being caused by demonic oppression, you will need to start taking authority over the works of the devil. As a disciple of Christ, you have already been given the power. Start the process of your deliverance with a simple two-part prayer. In the first part ask the Lord to set you free. Ask Jesus to destroy all the demonic devices and assignments that have been sent against you.

In the second part of the prayer, you will need to pray like Saint Paul: *One day, as we were going to the place of prayer, we met a slave-girl who had a spirit of divination and brought her owners a great deal of money by fortune-telling. While she followed Paul and us, she would cry out, "These men are slaves of the Most High God, who proclaim to you a way of salvation." She kept doing this for many days. But Paul, very much annoyed, turned and said to the spirit, "I order you in the name of Jesus Christ to come out of her." And it came out that very hour.*[18]

All during this time Paul had been praying to the Lord, but the demon only left the girl when he took authority over the situation by saying, *"I order you in the name of Jesus Christ."* There's a difference between asking God to make the devil go away and commanding it to leave in the name, power, and authority of Christ.

In order to move with the same power as Saint Paul, it will be necessary to start using both forms of prayer. After you ask God for his assistance, start using the power and authority that has been given to all disciples. Speak the words out loud, *I command you demonic spirits of infirmity to get out of my body. I break all agreements with you in the name of Jesus.*

If you have been blaming your heavenly Father for the works of the devil, take a minute right now to ask the Lord's forgiveness. God is a loving God who only desires your holiness, obedience, and well-being. God wants your intimate fellowship, and when you subconsciously blame him for disasters, accidents, sickness, and disease, it will harm your ability to commune with him in the way that he desires.

If you are a priest or lay-minister who has been preaching sermons about suffering that have not glorified God's loving character, take a minute right now and ask the Lord's forgiveness. Ask God to remove all unhealthy theology from your thought process and replace it with the truth. If you have tried to comfort a sick friend by telling them illness was their cross to bear, do whatever it takes to make amends for your actions.

Turn to your heavenly Father and offer him thanksgiving and praise for giving you power over all the works of the devil. Thank him for the angelic army that watches over you night and day. Your heavenly Father is a good and loving God who takes no pleasure in seeing anyone suffer. He is calling you right now to enter into a deeper and more passionate relationship with the Blessed Trinity.

Woe to you, scribes and Pharisees, hypocrites!
For you clean the outside of the cup and of the plate,
but inside they are full of greed and self-indulgence.
You blind Pharisee! First clean the inside of the cup,
so that the outside also may become clean.

Matthew 23:25–26

CHAPTER IV

Communion with Christ
Establishing an Authentic Relationship

Whoever, therefore, eats the bread or drinks the cup of the Lord in an unworthy manner will be answerable for the body and blood of the Lord. Examine yourselves, and only then eat of the bread and drink of the cup. For all who eat and drink without discerning the body, eat and drink judgment against themselves. For this reason many of you are weak and ill, and some have died.[2]

When the Church was first established, the Eucharistic celebration had so much power that if anyone received the Body and Blood in an unworthy manner, severe consequences were experienced. Instead of examining their hearts and taking into account the heavy price the Lord paid for the forgiveness of their sins, some of the Corinthians were getting drunk on the wine, while others went hungry. When this happened, the presence of Christ that was within the celebration, militated against the sinful nature that was present in the assembly, and some of them became sick, while others died.

As Church history continues to unfold and the religious spirits continue their assault, it would appear that the amount of power that is present in the Eucharist has greatly diminished. For many pre–Vatican II Catholics, the Eucharistic celebration was a serious time where the entire congregation fasted overnight.

Today, some parishioners attend Mass while drinking coffee, and others approach the Communion line chewing gum. Many Catholics haven't been to confession in years, and very few understand the Lord's redemptive work on the cross. According to the latest statistics, *only thirty-eight percent recognize the Real Presence of Jesus in the Eucharist. This is only slightly higher than a recent Gallup poll that found just thirty-three percent of today's Catholics believe in the Real Presence.*[3]

To counteract this problem, the Church has been dedicating more resources to the education of its parishioners. Many of our priests and deacons have been delivering homilies about the real presence of Christ in the Eucharist. I remember one sermon from a deacon at my parish. He engaged the audience with great enthusiasm, as he boldly proclaimed many of the profound truths found in the Catechism: *The Eucharist is the source and summit of the Christian life.*[4] *For in the blessed Eucharist is contained the whole spiritual good of the Church, namely Christ himself, our Pasch.*[5]

As I listened to his homily, it felt like Communion was the most profound encounter with God that I could ever experience. That if I wanted to receive the fullness of everything the Church had to offer, the source and summit of Christian life, then all I needed to do was walk up in the Communion line and receive the very presence of Christ himself.

As I looked around the congregation, I began to wonder about the lady who had been diagnosed with cancer. She has been going to Mass and receiving Communion for many years, and yet a deadly disease continues to attack her body. Does this mean Jesus wants her to suffer? When she receives the source and summit of Christian life, the actual Body and Blood of our Lord, and remains sick, does this mean the Lord doesn't want to heal her?

As I continued looking around the congregation, another couple came to mind. They had been married once before and were currently living together without an annulment. They too were receiving the Body, Blood, soul, and divinity of our Savior, yet it would appear the Lord had nothing to say about their situation. The Bible says that those who practice such things will not enter the kingdom of heaven. Yet when this couple receives Communion, it would appear the Lord remains silent.

As I continued looking at the people around me, I began to wonder why sixty-six percent of Catholics don't believe in the Real Presence of Christ in the Eucharist. Everybody in the congregation desperately needed a deeper encounter with the Lord, yet for some, it would appear that receiving Communion has become a rote routine. They go to Mass, sit, stand, kneel, receive their wafer, and within an hour, have fulfilled their Sunday obligation.

To correct this problem, the Church has been sending forth the clergy with the bold proclamation, *This is the actual Body and Blood of Christ*, but it doesn't seem to be helping. The source of the problem is not the Church's teachings, or the lack of education; the source of the problem lies within the hearts of those attending the service. The root of the problem is that many Catholics don't want to know Christ. Many don't feel worthy. Others don't want Jesus getting involved in their everyday affairs.

When an entire congregation shows up hungry to experience the Lord's presence, God will manifest himself in profound, life-changing ways. But when nobody wants the Lord, nobody feels worthy to encounter Jesus, nobody wants to sing his praises, nobody wants Jesus getting involved in their financial or sexual activities, then the Lord respects our free will and doesn't force his loving presence on anyone.

Before I could gain a deeper appreciation for the actual presence of Christ in the Eucharist, I first had to have an actual encounter with the risen Lord Jesus. I have been Catholic all my life, yet for many years, I lived a life devoid of God. I had been baptized as an infant, attended Catholic grade school, served as an altar boy, and was confirmed with my ninth-grade class. I participated in the Catholic religion to the best of my abilities, including serving as a lector and Eucharistic minister. God has always had his hand on my life, but it wasn't until my early adult years that I really started pursuing God. God had always been pursuing me, but before I could enter into a deep, rich, and passionate relationship with Christ, I first had to start pursuing him.

One of my first breakthroughs was the realization that the Catholic Church was not my God. That God is my God and it's the Church's job to connect me with the real God, not to become a false god unto me. After I realized that God is bigger than the Catholic Church and that God was calling me into a deeper union with himself, I then had the option to start pursuing him.

One of the ways I started pursuing God was to give up television for lent. At the time I had been attending daily Mass for at least five years. After working hard all day, I would come home and watch several hours of nonsense every evening on television. I didn't have cable, so I would flip channels around until my ten o'clock bedtime.

My purpose in giving up television for lent was to spend that time in prayer; but on Ash Wednesday, I could only pray for five minutes. I didn't know how to pray or commune with God. I only knew how to recite memorized prayers, so after praying as long as I could, I became bored and ended up going to bed around seven o'clock.

As the days of lent moved closer toward Easter, my love and relationship with the Lord began to blossom. Before long I couldn't wait for six o'clock to roll around. I would watch the clock with anxious anticipation, so that I could start the sacred ritual for the evening. After eating dinner, I would hang out with the Lord all night. I would take blankets outside, lie in my hammock, and talk to Jesus like my closest friend. It was a glorious time that gave birth to a passionate love affair.

Sometimes no words were necessary. I would just be with him, resting in his loving arms, looking up at the star-filled night sky. Sometimes I would ask questions, and the answers would arrive almost immediately. Other times I would only have to think a thought like, *Oh Lord, wouldn't it be nice if I could see a shooting…* Before I could finish the sentence, a bright streak of light shot across the night sky.

During these deep and profound encounters with God, I developed a desire to experience more of his loving presence. I wanted to experience the fullness of all that he had for me. After an actual encounter with the Lord, my spiritual eyes were opened and my heart longed for more. When my heart was hungry to receive the actual presence of Christ in my prayer time, I became even more eager to receive the actual presence of Christ in the Eucharist.

Another experience that made me more open to receive the fullness of the Lord's presence occurred while I was traveling with a friend named Julie. It was going to take us a full day to get back home. We had to drive several hours to return the rental car and then fly back to Denver with a one-hour layover in Houston. Somewhere during the trip we decided to pray, except this time we wanted our prayer to be different. Instead of repeating the words of rote routine over and over again, talking to Jesus like he was abstract and distant, we decided to pray from a more personal perspective.

In Matthew 18:20 Jesus says, *"For where two or three are gathered in my name, I am there among them."* As Julie and I were driving to the airport, we pictured Jesus in the backseat riding along with us. The more we brought this Scripture passage to life through the power of faith, the more it changed the way we prayed. This change came by realizing how much differently we would pray if Jesus really were traveling with us in the backseat of the car. Would we recite rote prayers over and over again, or talk to him like he was floating around in outer space?

Instead of praying in the manner typical to my upbringing, I started talking to Jesus like a dear friend. I started praying in the same way that Peter interacted with Jesus when they went fishing together. As you can imagine, the conversation was rich and deep. Julie and I prayed the entire way home. Before we knew it, the entire day had passed and it only seemed like thirty minutes. We communed with Jesus in the first person just as if he were traveling by our sides the entire time.

It was profound encounters such as these that made my experiences of receiving Communion at Mass even more exciting. When my heart was open to receive more of the Lord's loving presence throughout the entire day, it was even more open to receive the Lord in the most Holy Sacrifice of the Mass. When my heart was closed, or when I was cut off from God by living in sin, or when I was scared of God's wrath, or scared that he wanted to inflict punishment on me, those negative attitudes affected my ability to commune with him in a deep and meaningful manner.

This same principle applies to the entire congregation. When the hearts of God's children long for their heavenly Father, when the entire assembly can't wait to praise his holy name, hear his Word, and receive the fullness of his heavenly blessings, then the power of God shows up with incredible splendor. But when the vast majority of the congregation doesn't want anything to do with the Lord, and when they are only there to fulfill their Sunday obligations, then the service and the Eucharist lose power.

The only way to correct this problem is to correct the hearts of those attending the Eucharistic celebration. For the vast majority of Catholics, this will need to include a spiritual awakening. Many will need to experience an authentic encounter with the Lord. Once they do, they will become more hungry to experience and receive the actual presence of Christ in the Eucharist.

One of my first encounters with the actual presence of Christ in the Eucharist was when a friend of mine named Brenda asked me to cover her hour in the Adoration Chapel. At the time I was going to the bars on the weekend, and the hour she wanted me to cover was ten o'clock on Friday night.

"You can't be late," she said. "There's usually nobody else at that time. And the lady before me likes leaving on time."

At the time I had never even heard about the Adoration Chapel, but because Brenda was so persistent, I reluctantly agreed. I remember grumbling to myself on the way to the church. I was thinking how stupid it would be to sit in a room all by myself with a Eucharistic host on display for an hour, especially on Friday night when I could be out having fun at the nightclubs.

Because of my negative attitude, I managed to arrive late. I miscalculated the time it took to drive across town, and by the time I arrived, the lady before me had already left. I used the access code Brenda had given me to unlock the door and took a seat in the front row.

I was in there all by myself, still grumbling about how lame this was going to be, when all of a sudden the presence of the Lord came upon me like an armed warrior. It felt like a torrent of life-giving water had pinned me to the back of the chair. It was so powerful I started to cry. I just sat there in total awe, as the presence of the Lord filled the emptiness of my heart—the emptiness that I had been trying to fill in the bar scene.

It was so profound I didn't want to leave. Before I knew what hit me, a man unlocked the door and took a seat behind me. It was eleven o'clock, and from that point forward, I learned how powerful the divine presence of Christ is in the Eucharist.

I have sat in empty churches of other denominations, and it always feels like I'm sitting in an empty warehouse. Once all the people leave and the praise music comes to an end, any kind of supernatural presence ceases. When I sit alone in a Catholic Church late at night, I can feel the same supernatural presence that I encountered my first evening in the Adoration Chapel.

Instead of trying to convince Catholics that Christ is truly present in the Eucharist, the Church would be more successful encouraging Catholics to open up their hearts and experience the fullness of Christ that is already present in the Eucharist. One way that helped me open up my heart was to start participating in the Mass. I have found the more I cooperate with the Mass, the more I am able to receive from the Mass.

For many years, I have sat in the pew going through the motions. After attending daily Mass for over twenty years now, I realize there were many times when it had become a rote routine. After tasting the presence of the Lord and knowing that he is good, I now want to receive the fullness of all that God has for me. To do this, I started making a conscious effort to participate in the Mass. When the prayers of consecration are being said, instead of watching the priest pray, I started praying with him:

> *We come to you, Father, with praise and thanksgiving, through Jesus Christ your Son. Through him we ask you to accept and bless these gifts we offer you in sacrifice. We offer them for your holy Catholic Church, watch over it, Lord, and guide it; grant it peace and unity throughout the world.[6]*

During the prayer of consecration, the priest is praying on behalf of the congregation. That is why the text reads *we*. *We* offer to you this sacrifice of praise… *We* pray to you our loving and true God… Because the text says *we*, it includes everybody in the congregation. Because everybody is included in the prayer, it would be helpful if everybody started agreeing with the intentions behind the prayer.

When the priest asks for the bread and wine to become the Body and Blood of our Lord, I join with him in prayer. When I pray along with the prayers at Mass and join my spirit with the prayers, it opens up my heart to receive more of the divine presence of Christ that is present in the Eucharist. The same would also apply to everybody else in the congregation. Anytime anyone starts praying for Christ to be present in the Eucharist, they will be more open to experience and receive Christ in the Eucharist.

When the priest says, *"On the night he was betrayed,"*[7] I allow myself to be drawn into the upper room. On the night Jesus was betrayed, he celebrated the Last Supper with his disciples. *He broke the bread, gave it to his disciples, and said, "Take this, all of you, and eat it: this is my body which will be given up for you." When supper was ended, he took the cup. Again he gave you thanks and praise, gave the cup to his disciples, and said: "Take this, all of you, and drink from it: this is the cup of my blood, the blood of the new and everlasting covenant. It will be shed for you and for all so that sins may be forgiven."*[8]

As the words of consecration are being prayed, I allow myself to recline at the table with the other disciples. I picture what the upper room looked like. I allow myself to look into the Lord's eyes, as I watch him break the bread and pray a blessing over the cup. I allow myself to feel his love. I imagine what it was like to sit next to the Lord and rest my head against his chest like John did at the Last Supper.

When the priest says, *"Father, calling to mind the death your Son endured for our salvation,"*[9] I move through the upper room and begin the journey with the Lord toward the cross of Calvary. I picture the Lord walking through the darkness as he enters the garden of Gethsemane. Soon he will endure tremendous suffering as his flesh is torn apart from the lashes of the Roman soldiers. He will endure excruciating pain as nails are being driven through his hands and feet. He endured all this so that my sins could be forgiven, so that I could be reconciled to my heavenly Father.

To properly discern the Body and Blood of the Lord means to realize and accept the Lord's sacrifice that was made on the cross of Calvary. When we eat his Body that was broken under the weight of our sins, we are allowing the Lord to pay the penalty on our behalf. When we drink his Blood, we are allowing our sins to be placed on the cross at Calvary and are asking to be washed clean.

The next time you find yourself in front of the altar and are praying together with the priest saying, *"Therefore we offer you, God ever faithful and true, the sacrifice which restores man to your friendship,"*[10] remember to properly discern the Lord's sacrifice before receiving Holy Communion.

If you have been living in a state of mortal sin, it will be necessary to change your lifestyle and go to confession before receiving Communion. If you have offended your brother or sister, it will be necessary to leave your gift before the altar, *first be reconciled to your brother or sister, and then come and offer your gift.*[11] If you are struggling with serious problems or difficulties in life, the Lord wants to have a very long and deep conversation with you after receiving Communion.

He is calling you right now. Please don't spend a lifetime practicing religious behaviors devoid of a passionate relationship with Christ. Come to know him before it's too late. One man named Phil waited his entire lifetime before entering into an authentic relationship with Jesus. He attended Church every Sunday, but as he grew older, he sensed that his time had come to pass from this world to the next.

He went to see his pastor and asked, "Will you please teach me how to pray?"

The priest went to his library, and after looking around, he pulled out a heavy textbook. He handed it to Phil and said, "You should be able to find everything you need in here."

Phil took the book home with excitement. The next day he returned it to the parish office. His pastor said, "How did you read that so fast?"

"I couldn't get through the first few pages," Phil said. "I don't understand all the theological terms. I just want to know how to pray."

Upon hearing the conversation, an associate pastor offered Phil some advice. "All you need to do is go home and set up an empty chair. After you invite Jesus to join you, start speaking to him as if he were sitting in the chair directly in front of you."

Phil went home with a mission. He immediately set up a chair in his bedroom, and within a short time, he developed a passionate relationship with the

Lord. When his time came to pass from this world to the next, his family and distant relatives gathered around his bedside. Phil would oftentimes be short of breath, but whenever anyone tried to sit in that chair, Phil would rise up and say, "Please don't sit there!"

On the day Phil went home to be with the Lord, in his dying moments he used his last bit of strength to crawl out of bed and rest his head in the chair. No one in Phil's family understood what was going on until the young priest conducted his funeral.

When one of Phil's grandchildren asked about the chair in Phil's bedroom, the priest said, "That is where the Lord used to sit and speak with your grandpa before he went to be with him for all eternity."

Do you know Jesus on a deep, personal, and intimate level? Are you communing with the lover of your soul on a daily basis? Have you accepted the Lord's sacrifice on the cross for the forgiveness of your sins? Are you properly discerning the Body and Blood of Christ every time you receive Communion?

If you have fallen into a stagnant pattern of attending Mass without any real desire to commune with God on a deep, intimate, and personal level, take a moment right now to ask the Lord's forgiveness. Ask Jesus to come into your life in a very real and profound way.

If you have been receiving the Body and Blood of the Lord in an unworthy manner, allow the words from Saint Paul to penetrate your heart. *"Whoever, therefore, eats the bread or drinks the cup of the Lord in an unworthy manner will be answerable for the body and blood of the Lord."*[12] Keep in mind that when one member of the body suffers, the rest of the body is affected. If after examining your conscious you find yourself falling short, take a moment right now to make amends.

Why not take some time today to set up an empty chair in your home and start communing with the Lord on an exciting new dimension? Ask for the grace to abstain from television and all other noisy distractions in your life. Start spending your evenings communing with the great lover of your soul. Make a commitment to start pursuing Jesus, the most Holy Sacrifice of the altar, in all your endeavors.

The Father who sent me
has himself testified on my behalf.
You have never heard his voice or seen his form,
and you do not have his word abiding in you,
because you do not believe him whom he has sent.
You search the scriptures because you think
that in them you have eternal life;
and it is they that testify on my behalf.
Yet you refuse to come to me to have life.

John 5:37–40

Surrender Your Life to the Lord Following in Complete Obedience

The ultimate end of the whole divine economy is the entry of God's creatures into the perfect unity of the Blessed Trinity. But even now we are called to be a dwelling for the Most Holy Trinity: "If a man loves me," says the Lord, "he will keep my word, and my Father will love him, and we will come to him, and make our home with him."[2]

According to the Catechism, the entire purpose of our existence is to come into perfect unity with the Blessed Trinity. Jesus wants to come and make his home deep inside the spiritual temple of every baptized believer. God is love, and he wants to establish an authentic relationship with all of his beloved children.

The way to develop an intimate relationship with the Blessed Trinity is a lifelong process. It is not a one-time event like Baptism, and it doesn't occur by saying a simple prayer to receive salvation. The seeds that we plant in this lifetime will reap an eternal harvest in the next. The way we live our lives in this generation will have a direct effect on our eternal existence.

If we surrender our lives into the Lord's service and allow our hearts to be transformed by the power of his Holy Spirit, then we will be welcomed into an eternal relationship with the Blessed Trinity. If we live a lifetime devoid of his Holy Spirit and distant from the Lord's fellowship, regardless of the amount of religious behaviors that we perform, according to the words of Christ, we may end up being separated from him for all eternity:

When the Son of Man comes in his glory, and all the angels with him, then he will sit on the throne of his glory. All the nations will be gathered before him, and he will separate people one from another as a shepherd separates the sheep from the goats, and he will put the sheep at his right hand and the goats at the left.[3]

Then the king will say to those at his right hand, "Come, you that are blessed by my Father, inherit the kingdom prepared for you from the foundation of the world; for I was hungry and you gave me food, I was thirsty and you gave me something to drink, I was a stranger and you welcomed me, I was naked and you gave me clothing, I was sick and you took care of me, I was in prison and you visited me."[4]

Then the sheep will respond to the Lord by saying, *"Lord, when was it that we saw you hungry and gave you food, or thirsty and gave you something to drink?" And the king will answer them, "Truly I tell you, just as you did it to one of the least of these who are members of my family, you did it to me."[5]*

Then the King will say to the goats, *"You that are accursed, depart from me into the eternal fire prepared for the devil and his angels; for I was hungry and you gave me no food, I was thirsty and you gave me*

*nothing to drink, I was a stranger and you did not wel-
come me, naked and you did not give me clothing, sick
and in prison and you did not visit me."[6]*

On the surface, it would appear the only difference between the sheep and goats are a few random
acts of kindness, but the underlying difference is obedience. Sheep are submissive. Goats are rebellious.
Sheep follow the Good Shepherd. Goats are stubborn, always wanting their own way. The transformation process between the sheep and the goats begins
with an authentic relationship with the Good
Shepherd.

Jesus says, *"Very truly, I tell you, I am the gate for
the sheep. All who came before me are thieves and ban-
dits; but the sheep did not listen to them. I am the gate.
Whoever enters by me will be saved, and will come in
and go out and find pasture. The thief comes only to
steal and kill and destroy. I came that they may have
life, and have it abundantly."[7]*

*"I am the good shepherd. The good shepherd lays
down his life for the sheep. The hired hand, who is not
the shepherd and does not own the sheep, sees the wolf
coming and leaves the sheep and runs away—and the
wolf snatches them and scatters them. The hired hand
runs away because a hired hand does not care for the
sheep. I am the good shepherd. I know my own and my
own know me, just as the Father knows me and I know
the Father."[8]*

Jesus is the Good Shepherd who loves and cares
for his flock. The hired hands are those who tend the
flock on his behalf. When the wolf comes, most of us

would rather run away to save our own lives. The wolf is the devil, and his destructive armies of religious spirits have only one purpose—to steal, kill, and destroy.

Because of the effects of original sin, we are all born rebellious goats. To enter the Lord's flock, we will need to die to our fleshly, goat-driven desires and become like obedient sheep. We will need to denounce the devil's lies and submit ourselves unto the service of the Good Shepherd as obedient sheep. The transformation process from our goat-like characteristics is a lifelong journey, but at some point there will need to be a place of full and complete surrender.

Before I was willing to surrender my life to the Lord, I had to experience a devastating financial loss. At the time, I was twenty-eight years old and had spent the previous six years of my life buying HUD houses, fixing them up, and selling them. I could see real estate prices rising, so I bought land for a townhouse project. The property was located on the third fairway of a golf course, and one of the foundations had already been poured. The previous developer had declared bankruptcy, so I was able to acquire the land at a great price.

I worked twelve to fourteen hours a day building town homes for nearly two years. After I sold the last unit, I considered myself financially retired. All I needed to do was invest my money in the stock market, and I could live comfortably off the interest for the rest of my life.

Instead of investing my money in stocks and bonds, I found myself drawn to the commodity market. I had discovered a trading system where I could earn over two hundred percent a year. I tested the system for several months on paper. Some days it would lose money, but over all, it produced great results.

I was so confident in the trading system that I committed all my time to the markets. Within the first week I made ten thousand dollars, but after that, the market turned against me. After experiencing my first major loss, I started getting worried. I didn't want to sell my position and accept the loss, because the market could turn around at any time. The longer I waited, the more it moved against me. I had been trading in denial. It hurt so bad I could barely function. Every waking moment I was in agony, until one day I had to accept the loss of more than a quarter of a million dollars.

I was totally devastated. I couldn't eat or sleep, so at the advice of my pastor, I decided to go on retreat. After packing a bag, I drove up to Estes Park. I was furious at myself and at God for inspiring me with the trading system in the first place. I felt God had let me down. I had been planning on giving God forty percent of all the trading profits.

In the past, I had faithfully tithed ten percent of my income, and ever since I started tithing, God had abundantly blessed the work of my hands. Now that I wanted to increase my tithe from ten percent to forty percent, God allowed me to lose $250,000.00. He didn't even bother warning me. I wanted to give back to God for all that he had given me, and look at where it got me, broken and devastated.

After checking my bags into the retreat facility, I laced up my hiking boots and blasted up the tallest mountain peak available. I crashed my way through trees, across flowing streams, and over large rock formations. Upon reaching the top, I wanted to have it out with the Almighty—but there was nothing but the sound of sheer silence.

It felt like when I needed God the most he was nowhere to be found. After about an hour, I returned to my room broken and crushed. Laying face-down on the floor crying, in the unspoken words of my heart, I surrendered my life to God by saying, *I will do whatever you want from here on out.* As soon as I surrendered my life to the Lord, God showed up like a bolt of lightning. He filled my heart with peace and gave me my first assignment—to write a book.

It was like the difference between night and day. One minute I was crushed and devastated, the next, I was filled with joy and peace. In that moment of surrender, I was transformed from being a stubborn, self-willed goat into an obedient sheep. I had been Catholic my whole life. At the time of my stock market loss, I had been attending daily Mass for at least ten years. I was doing everything everybody else was doing, including tithing ten percent of my income, but I had never surrendered my life into the Lord's service.

In that moment of surrender, I went from being self-employed to God-employed. When I was self-employed, I would pray for God to bless my endeavors, *O please God, I want to make money building town homes. O please God, help me do this and that.*

If was all about *me*—I wanted God to fulfill *my* plans. After I surrendered my life into the Lord's service, it was all about God—whatever God wanted me to do, I would be obedient and accept. If God wanted me to go to Africa, live in a tent, and preach the Gospel to villagers, I would go and be obedient. If God wanted me to live as a celibate monk, I would be obligated to surrender my self-willed ways and submit to the Lord's plans.

This is the major difference between the sheep and the goats. The goats go to church for an hour on Sunday, yet they follow their own dreams, plans, and desires. They don't know the Good Shepherd's voice, and they have never surrendered their lives into his service. The sheep know how to listen to the voice of the Good Shepherd. When the Lord calls them into ministry, they are obedient and produce fruit for the kingdom of heaven.

Jesus says, *"My sheep hear my voice. I know them, and they follow me."*[9] This is a critical requirement for being part of the Lord's flock. The sheep are required to listen to the voice of the Good Shepherd. They are required to hear his voice, to discern the difference between God's voice and all the other voices in the world, and to follow in complete obedience.

After God called me to write a book, I drove back home the next day filled with joy. It took me two years to complete my first assignment. During that time, I learned how to listen to the voice of the Good Shepherd. At first I didn't know what I was doing, because no one had taught me how to listen and discern the softly spoken voice of the Lord.

After surrendering my life unto the Lord's service, my first tendency was to complete the book assignment and present it back to God when it was finished. Almost like a little child would say, *I'm going to do this all by myself…don't touch…keep away.* Soon, I realized that God wanted to help me write the book. He wanted us to work on the project together. Before I could work together with the Lord on a daily basis, I first needed to know how to listen to the voice of the Good Shepherd.

I started this process in the Adoration Chapel. First, I had to quiet my mind. Next, I had to remove all the noise and confusion that was running around inside my head. During this process, all kinds of distractions would arise, but after learning the necessary disciplines of contemplative prayer, I started to hear the voice of the Holy Spirit that resided deep within my soul more clearly.

The Catechism says, *Contemplative prayer is hearing the Word of God. Far from being passive, such attentiveness is the obedience of faith, the unconditional acceptance of a servant, and the loving commitment of a child.*[10]

Contemplative prayer seeks him "whom my soul loves." It is Jesus, and in him, the Father. We seek him, because to desire him is always the beginning of love, and we seek him in that pure faith which causes us to be born of him and to live in him.[11]

Contemplative prayer is silence, the "symbol of the world to come" or "silent love." Words in this kind of prayer are not speeches; they are like kindling that feeds the fire of love.[12]

Not only does contemplative prayer involve a lot of practice, but it also requires a lot of discipline. Our world is so filled with noise and distraction that it's almost impossible for most people to spend five minutes in silence. Everywhere we go noisy advertisements are jumping out at us. Grocery and department stores have music playing in the background, we listen to the radio in our cars, and most Americans watch more than two hours of television every evening.

After surrendering my life into the Lord's service, it became necessary for me to hear from the Good Shepherd on a daily basis. Once I completed my first assignment, I had to run back to the Lord to get more instructions for the next assignment. From the moment I surrendered my life to the Lord, I have been constantly praying, *what do you want me to do next?* There were many times when I had to sit in silence and wait for hours for the Lord to speak.

On one occasion I felt stuck. My first book had been published, and I found myself sitting around asking the Lord what he wanted me to do next. It felt like my life had been put on hold. Eventually I started getting angry, and in my arrogance I said, *Here I am a successful real estate developer, who has owned everything from a car dealership to an eighteen-bay body shop, and here you have me sitting around doing nothing.*

Once I surrendered my life unto the Lord's service, I meant it with every fiber of my being. I kept pursuing God until he gave me my next assignment. Then one day as I was practicing contemplative prayer in the Adoration Chapel, the inspiration that came to me was shocking—I felt the Lord calling me to live on the streets for a weekend. I didn't hear any audible words, but I knew in my heart the Lord wanted me to experience what it was like to be homeless.

After the Lord had spoken, I had a choice to make—was I going to be obedient, or would I pretend that I hadn't heard the voice of the Lord? Part of the discernment process in contemplative prayer comes from distinguishing among the voice of God, the voice of the devil, and the voice of my own fleshly desires. Many times all three voices seem so confusing that it's hard to know when God is speaking.

In this case, I knew the prompting to spend a weekend living on the streets wasn't coming from my own fleshly desires. My flesh liked living in my safe, warm, comfortable house. The voice didn't sound like it was coming from the devil either. The devil usually speaks to me in a tone of fear-driven negativity or the voice of some other self-gratifying temptation. After taking the time to discern the spirits to make sure the Lord was calling me to live on the streets for a weekend, I set out for the adventure of a lifetime.

It was during the middle of winter, so I dressed in my warmest clothes. I bought an old sleeping bag from a thrift store and packed some bottles of water in an army duffel bag. I also took along some cardboard signs. After parking my truck at my parents' house, I left my cell phone behind and started walking toward the downtown area.

I didn't bring any money with me, so after reaching the first intersection, I pulled out my cardboard signs to see what would happen. One sign said, *I need $5 to eat today.* I stood at that intersection for over an hour, and nobody gave me anything. Nobody would even look at me. It was the most humbling and humiliating experience that I have ever encountered. There I was, an accomplished, self-employed, real estate developer, who had owned numerous businesses with great financial success, holding a cardboard sign trying to bum a few bucks.

After a few hours, I sat down in the grass totally discouraged. I didn't think I would be able to last an entire weekend. After suffering through the frustration of trying to do things my own way, I decided to pray. As soon as I did, a lady in a small car honked her horn at me. She rolled down her window and said, "Do you need some money?"

She was waving cash out her car window, so I jumped up and ran across the street. She handed me six dollars. It was all the money that I needed for the day. I was overjoyed. I was able to ride the bus downtown and spent the rest of the weekend ministering to the people that I met on the streets.

The weekend turned out to be the birth of my homeless ministry. By calling me to live on the streets, the Lord taught me great humility and a deep compassion for the homeless. Before, I had no compassion for the guys holding cardboard signs. I had no idea what it was like to live on the streets without experiencing it firsthand. Before the Lord could call me into ministry, he first needed to train me with a real-life experience.

The transformation process between the sheep and the goats started with my obedience. First, I needed to surrender my life into the Lord's hands. Next, I needed to sit in silence practicing contemplative prayer. After hearing from the Lord, I needed to proceed with complete obedience. It was through this three-part process that I overcame my selfish goat-like tendencies and became an obedient sheep.

It was through this process that I was able to feed the hungry, clothe the naked, and welcome the stranger. It was through this process that I was obedient to the Lord's command, *"Truly I tell you, just as you did it to one of the least of these who are members of my family, you did it to me."*[13] Without the knowledge that Jesus actually wanted to have an authentic, life-changing relationship with me, without the complete surrender of my life into the Lord's hands, without the obedience of listening to the Good Shepherd's voice, none of this would have been possible.

My ability to listen to the voice of the Good Shepherd has grown tremendously over the years. One of the great advancements came the day I

removed the television from my house. The more I
started communing with God, the more the television
set started interfering with my spirituality. I noticed
that when I spent two hours at night praying to God,
I felt more empowered and spiritually charged the
next day. When I spent two hours watching television
in the evening, I usually felt lustful, greedy, materialistic, and spiritually drained the next day.

As time went on I started watching less television, but there were times when I would come home
from work, and all I wanted to do was make dinner
and relax by watching a movie. But every time I did,
it robbed me. Two hours of prayer with the Lord
charged me; two hours of television drained and discouraged me.

Knowing that there was nothing on the television that could ever compare with spending two
hours with the Lord, I would unplug the television
and make a commitment never to watch it again.
Then in my weakness, I would plug it back in. After
plugging and unplugging the television set for several
months, I completely removed it from my house. I
took my entertainment center apart, put the television and stereo equipment in a box, and turned that
room into a prayer chapel. It has been one of the best
moves I ever made to increase my ability to hear from
the Lord.

Was there ever a time when you surrendered
your life in complete obedience to the Lord? Do you
consider the Lord your Master? Have you become his
good and faithful servant? Many times we call Jesus
our Lord with the words of our prayers, but have you

actually made Jesus the Lord of your life?

Jesus says, *"Why do you call me 'Lord, Lord,' and do not do what I tell you? I will show you what someone is like who comes to me, hears my words, and acts on them. That one is like a man building a house, who dug deeply and laid the foundation on rock; when a flood arose, the river burst against that house but could not shake it, because it had been well built. But the one who hears and does not act is like a man who built a house on the ground without a foundation. When the river burst against it, immediately it fell, and great was the ruin of that house."*[14]

If you have never surrendered your life into the Lord's service, take a minute right now and give him your full obedience. Surrender the direction and purpose of your life into his hands. Turn from your self-employed ways and become God-employed. Repent for all the times you have acted like a disobedient goat instead of a faithful little lamb.

If you have been spending more time watching television and listening to music than you have been communing with the lover of your soul, ask the Lord's forgiveness and make a commitment to change your ways. Ask for the grace to remove anything from your life, home, and environment that hinders your ability to commune with the Good Shepherd. Start listening to his softly spoken words in the quiet stillness of your heart.

You must understand this,
that in the last days
distressing times will come.
For people will be lovers of themselves,
lovers of money, boasters, arrogant, abusive,
disobedient to their parents, ungrateful,
unholy, inhuman, implacable, slanderers,
profligates, brutes, haters of good, treacherous,
reckless, swollen with conceit, lovers of pleasure
rather than lovers of God,
holding to the outward form of godliness
but denying its power.

2 Timothy 3:1–5

CHAPTER VI

Removing the Devil's Devices
Entering into the Lord's Presence

Now the serpent was more crafty than any other wild animal that the Lord God had made. He said to the woman, "Did God say, 'You shall not eat from any tree in the garden'?" The woman said to the serpent, "We may eat of the fruit of the trees in the garden; but God said, 'You shall not eat of the fruit of the tree that is in the middle of the garden, nor shall you touch it, or you shall die.'"[2]

Once the devil planted the device of doubt and tempted Adam and Eve to sin, they became separated from their Creator. God being pure light, love, and truth could no longer unite with the presence of darkness. God's beloved children were expelled from the garden and sent away from the presence of the Lord.

The same situation continues today. From the dawn of creation the devil's purpose has been to prevent God's children from authentically connecting with their heavenly Father. God desperately desires to commune with all of his beloved children, but once the devil plants a device in our lives, we may find ourselves cut off from the presence of the Lord—unable to hear his voice.

DEVICE I

The main device that the devil uses is sin. Sin always separates men from God. A good example of how sin was able to cut me off from the presence of the Lord came one day when I was speeding. At the time I owned a black Corvette, and I always had to be the fastest car on the road. It made me feel powerful cutting in and out of traffic, passing everybody else.

As I was racing down the highway, God told me to drive the speed limit. I heard his voice as clear as day. Immediatcly, I slowed down and merged into the center lane. The only problem with driving the speed limit was that cars started backing up behind me. I could feel the impatient rush of the other motorists as they flew past me, cutting me off like I was an offensive object blocking their path.

A few days later, I reverted back to my old driving habits. Once again, I heard the voice of the Lord telling me to drive the speed limit. I tried with all my strength to be obedient, but after a week of being harassed by the other motorists, I decided that it would be acceptable with the Lord if I just kept up with traffic. That way I wouldn't be inconveniencing anybody else behind me.

This became a problem because everybody on the highway was driving ten miles an hour over the posted limit. As I continued to keep up with the traffic, the peaceful presence of the Lord that normally resides deep within my heart slowly faded away. At first I didn't even know the Lord's presence was gone, but within a week, it felt like I was suffering a severe spiritual famine.

I missed the Lord's presence so much that I was willing to do anything to get him back. A friend of mine gave me a Scripture passage concerning my situation, so I went to church and began to humble myself before the crucifix. I got down on my knees and begged God to show me the problem. The Scripture my friend gave me was from Proverbs 2:1–5.

My child, if you accept my words and treasure up my commandments within you, making your ear attentive to wisdom and inclining your heart to understanding; if you indeed cry out for insight, and raise your voice for understanding; if you seek it like silver, and search for it as for hidden treasures—then you will understand the fear of the Lord and find the knowledge of God.

After reading this passage several times, I started crying out for insight. *O Lord, please incline my heart to understand, speak to me clearly, make my ears attentive to your wisdom.* After about twenty minutes, I still wasn't hearing anything and began growing frustrated. In my arrogance I started telling the Lord how I have kept all his commandments. Eventually, I humbled myself again and asked the Lord a simple question. *What commandments haven't I kept?* As soon as I asked that question, the peaceful presence of the Lord returned to me and said, *If you can't drive the speed limit, sell the Corvette!*

After leaving the chapel that day, I immediately started driving the speed limit because I knew God was extremely serious. When the sign read 55, I set the cruise control for exactly that speed. It was almost unbearable at times. Every time I looked at the speedometer, I had to slow down. Cars would rush around me in an impatient fury. It took every bit of my strength to remain in control and obedient.

My breaking point came the day I was late for an appointment. The highway was wide open, and there I was driving 55 mph in my late-model Corvette. I wanted to please the Lord with every fiber of my being, but I had to start speeding because I didn't want to be late for my appointment. My heart was torn in sheer agony. The Lord had given me one simple assignment, and I couldn't do it. In my frustration, I started crying and pounding on the steering wheel.

In that moment of complete brokenness, I surrendered my inability to the Lord. As soon as I did, God showed up and supernaturally gave me the grace that I needed. I still have it to this very day. In that moment of surrender, God filled my heart with peace and placed a protective barrier around my vehicle. From that moment forward, the other motorists have been flowing around me as smooth as a gentle breeze. The angry, impatient rush that I used to experience completely disappeared.

Before this encounter, God was being gracious to me, even though I was rushing around, breaking laws, and endangering other motorists. Because of his great love, he needed to convict me of my sinfulness and call me to a deeper level of holiness. He probably could foresee a devastating accident in my future and wanted to save my life. He also wanted me to be filled with the fruits of the Holy Spirit at all times—peace, patience, joy, and self-control.

I'm sure the Lord had many other reasons for

asking me to drive the speed limit, including obedience to his written Word: *For the Lord's sake accept the authority of every human institution,³ and let every person be subject to the governing authorities; for there is no authority except from God, and those authorities that exist have been instituted by God.⁴*

This situation can also be viewed from the devil's perspective. All during this time, the devil had been encouraging my sin of pride, making me feel powerful as I cut in and out of traffic. The devil wanted me to cause the biggest accident possible, one where many lives would be devastated. He also wanted to fill me with stress, anxiety, and road rage, anything except the fruits and gifts of the Holy Spirit.

The devil knows that the Spirit of God cannot dwell inside a man when he's full of pride and impatience. Hence the devil was using the device of sin to cut me off from the presence of God. By choosing the devil's lies over God's truth, and living a lifetime under this kind of deception, it would have become very difficult for me to hear anything from the Lord.

DEVICE II

Another device the devil uses to cut people off from the presence of God is disobedience. If I had told God, *No! I don't want to drive the speed limit!* Then I would have been living in a state of constant sin, and that sin would have the power to separate me from God.

When the sin of disobedience is present in our lives, we usually don't want to hear what the Lord has to say. We are usually scared to ask for more clarity, so we pull away from prayer, hoping that God will forget about the idea. *Like somehow it will all go away and that God will allow us to bow out gracefully.* After a few weeks pass, we may try to reconnect with the Lord in prayer and then wonder why he remains silent.

When the sin of disobedience is present, God will remain silent until we get down on our knees and ask for his forgiveness. Once we repent, go back and accomplish what God has asked us to do in the first place, only then we will be reunited to his peaceful presence. If you want the presence of the living God to follow you around wherever you go, learn to say *yes! Yes God, I will do that right away! O yes Lord, I will take care of that immediately! O Yes God, whatever you want!*

DEVICE III

Another deadly device the devil uses to cut men off from the presence of God is the lack of forgiveness. When I first started practicing contemplative prayer, I made a commitment to spend an hour a day in the Adoration Chapel. After I cleared my mind of all the distracting thoughts, I was able to hear from the Lord as clear as day.

On other occasions, I would try to enter the Lord's presence, and all of a sudden, sick thoughts and feelings would arise from my past. At first I tried to push them back down. They were very negative—like the time a bully at school hurt me, or when I felt betrayed by coworkers, neighbors, and past girl-friends. I tried to disassociate myself from these thoughts and get back to the peaceful, loving presence of Christ, but then I finally realized that God was bringing these thoughts to the surface because he wanted me to forgive those people.

Jesus says, *"For if you forgive others their trespasses, your heavenly Father will also forgive you; but if you do not forgive others, neither will your Father forgive your trespasses."⁵* Both Ephesians 4:27 and the second Book of Corinthians 2:11 identify the lack of forgiveness as one of Satan's devices. The lack of forgiveness is like a deadly disease trapped inside the recesses of your soul. God wants to occupy every aspect of our hearts with his love, truth, and beauty, but when we choose to hold on to a grudge, we are using our free will to embrace one of the devil's devices.

The devil knows God's Spirit cannot dwell inside of a person when anger, resentment, and the lack of forgiveness are present. To get free from this bondage, we need to release our hurts to the Lord by making forgiveness an act of our free will. Once we ask for the Lord's grace to forgive, God will gladly come into our hearts and remove the devil's devices so that his loving presence can once again dwell inside of us.

DEVICE IV

Another snare the devil uses to cut people off from the presence of God is addictions. It's possible to become addicted to almost anything that we turn to for pleasure or comfort. Jesus wants to take the highest priority in our hearts, but when we say *No* to the Lord and *Yes* to our worldly pleasures, they can become false gods to us.

A good example of this comes from the life of an alcoholic. Instead of turning to God for love and comfort, an alcoholic turns to the bottle. When this happens, the demons that have been assigned to his life start interfering with his thoughts, leading him deeper into bondage. The same is true with any type of mood-altering medications.

There's no difference in God's eyes between getting high on illegal street drugs and getting high on prescription medications. Any type of mood-altering substance has the ability to hinder your relationship with God. It's not possible to commune with the Lord from the depths of your heart at the same time that you are drinking, getting high, or compulsively craving another cigarette. All addictions are harmful because any time a drug addict, smoker, or alcoholic tries to connect with the heart of Christ, the devil comes and pokes that person's inner wounds in an attempt to stir up more fleshly cravings.

Most addicts have been running from their childhood wounds their entire life. Instead of turning to the Lord for freedom, they have been turning to their addictions to make themselves feel better. To break this cycle, it will be necessary to resist the devil's temptations and allow the Lord's love to minister to every area of your past where you have been hurt. So long as we choose to turn to food, sex, alcohol, pornography, gambling, caffeine, nicotine, talk radio, television, or prescription medications, instead of turning to the Lord, they can become false gods to us and a snare to our ability to commune with the heart of Christ.

DEVICE V

Another snare the devil likes using is the sin of idolatry. The sin of idolatry cuts people off from God the same as addictions. All idols are false gods that we set up in our hearts that keep us away from the Lord. Jesus says, *"No one can serve two masters; for a slave will either hate the one and love the other, or be devoted to the one and despise the other. You cannot serve God and wealth."*[6]

At one point in my past, God allowed me to make a lot of money in real estate. At the time I thought I was being very religious, but after losing a quarter of a million dollars trading commodities, I realized that money had been my god. If someone had confronted me and accused me of serving the false god of money, I would have responded by saying, *I have been going to daily Mass for the past ten years. I tithe ten percent of my income. I say prayers every day. I'm doing more than most Catholics will ever do. How dare you accuse me of serving the false god of money?*

It was only after surrendering my life to the Lord that I realized money had become a false god. Looking back, I used to work twelve to fourteen hours a day to acquire money, yet only prayed fifteen minutes a day. When it came time to make decisions, I didn't ask the Lord's guidance. I never wanted the Lord's fairness and generosity when it came time to negotiate a contract. I made my decisions based on profit. I hired and fired employees like disposable work units. I had very little concern for anyone except myself.

Not only were my daily decisions based on money, but the larger direction of my life was focused on the pursuit of money. I never asked the Lord what he wanted me to do with my time. *O Lord, should I make money working real estate, or should I be serving the homeless?* Sure, I prayed to God every day, but never once did I surrender my life unto his service. Never once did I base my financial decisions on godly principles.

After losing a fortune trading commodities, I soon realized how I had been serving the false god of money for most of my life. After I surrendered my life into the Lord's service, I discovered the true meaning of putting the Lord's will first. Instead of working to make money every day, I started working to please the Lord. Instead of trying to acquire a bigger house, the Lord wanted me to sell my house and start serving the homeless. Instead of driving unproductive workers off my job site, the Lord wanted me to start driving homeless men around town helping them to find jobs.

DEVICE VI

The sin of idolatry also affected my relationships in the same way. When I would meet a beautiful girl, I didn't ask the Lord's permission to date her. Instead of making Jesus the Lord of my dating activities, I chose to follow my own fleshly desires.

On one occasion, after I met a tall beautiful blonde, the Holy Spirit kept screaming at me, *No!* I could feel the Spirit's conviction for weeks until finally I said, *Shut up, I want her!* I don't remember if I spoke the words out loud or just with the anger of my heart. It didn't matter. Once I told God, *No! I don't want your will for my life!* The Spirit of God departed from me.

After our breakup, I was emotionally devastated for several months. I remember lying on the floor, crying out to God, and repenting of my actions, when all of a sudden the Holy Spirit came rushing back, filling me with new life again. The Spirit's departure was so subtle that I didn't even know his presence was gone until he came rushing back. It was only then that I realized what had happened. I had committed the sin of idolatry. I had put the love of a woman over the Lord's will for my life.

DEVICE VII

It's also possible to commit the sin of idolatry by praying to spiritual entities other than God. The catechism says, *An idolater is someone who "transfers his indestructible notion of God to anything other than God."* In the spirit realm there are only two forces at work in the world—God and the devil. When we start praying to objects, people, canonized saints, spirit guides, or statues, as if they were God, or with the same reverence, devotion, and love that is due God alone, then we open ourselves up to demonic attack.

A good example of this comes from the Ouija board. When a young man starts calling out to spiritual entities other than the Blessed Trinity, demonic spirits have the right to answer his prayer requests. Demons are not bound to the semantics of names. They can change their names anytime they want.

When the young man calls out to the spirits of the dead, spirits of nature, or the spirit of his deceased Aunt Millie, the demons have the right to open up a direct line of communication with him.

The same is true for anyone who commits the sin of idolatry. It doesn't matter if you are seeking oracles from the dead through canonized saints, the Queen of Heaven, or the spiritual forces in the heavenly places; if you commit the sin of idolatry in your religious behaviors, then demonic spirits of religion will have the right to interfere with your spirituality. Once you allow religious spirits into your life, they will do everything in their power to cut you off from an authentic relationship with the Lord.

Take a look inside your heart and see if there's anything holding you back from a deeper relationship with the Lord. You should be able to sit down in prayer and within the first fifteen minutes be able to enter the Lord's presence. Try spending the next fifteen minutes centering yourself in God's presence by using a combination of prayer, praise, and worship. Then spend the rest of the time in silence to see if you are able to commune with the Lord from the depths of your heart.

When most people try the fifteen-minute test, all kinds of distractions arise. The phone may start ringing, or a fight will break out between the kids. Before you begin, you may want to eliminate as many distractions as possible. Dedicate the next fifteen minutes to the Lord. Turn off the television, radio, and telephone to see if you can pass the test by listening to the voice of the Good Shepherd.

After beginning this exercise, you may start to experience anxiety rising up in your heart. Maybe you have just eaten dinner, and as you start to pray, an overwhelming desire to eat something sweet comes over you. If you are experiencing any of these kinds of distractions, simply surrender them to the Lord and ask him to remove them from you.

If these feelings of anxiety continue to interfere with your prayer time, you can also rebuke them in the name of Jesus. Just say the words out loud, *In the name, power, and authority of Jesus, I rebuke you craving desires. In the name of Jesus, I command anything evil or demonic that is trying to interfere with my prayer time to leave my presence immediately.*

It may also be helpful to picture yourself resting in a peaceful environment. If you like the beach, allow yourself to hear the ocean and feel the warmth of the sun on your face. Picture what Jesus would look like if he walked over and sat down next to you. Look into his loving eyes. Talk to him as if he were your closest friend.

Once you are able to enter into the Lord's presence, ask Jesus if there are any unconfessed sins or any changes in your life that he would like you to make. Ask the Lord to show you any areas where you have been disobedient. If anything comes to mind, take the necessary time to repent and make amends for your actions.

If the Lord shows you any unhealthy behaviors, make a commitment to change your ways. Ask for the necessary grace to overcome that area with his grace.

If the Lord is calling you to drive the speed limit or to stop smoking, you may not have the ability without his help. If this is the case, take the necessary time to surrender your inability and ask for the necessary strength to be set free.

If the Lord shows you an unhealthy relationship that you are currently involved with, ask for the grace to surrender that person into the Lord's hands. Maybe you have been married once or twice before without the Lord's permission. If the Church has not joined you together in holy matrimony, then you may not be free to remarry without receiving an annulment.

If you are living with a man or woman who is not your God-approved spouse, then the sin of fornication will have the ability to separate you from the Lord's presence. If this is the case, ask for the necessary grace and guidance. After you surrender everything into the Lord's loving hands, start taking the necessary steps to follow Jesus in complete obedience from this day forward.

If you are not able to enter into the Lord's presence within the first fifteen minutes, keep working at it until you break through. Don't allow the devil's devices to hold you back. Jesus loves you, and he desperately desires to commune with all his beloved children. Step-by-step, the Lord will lead and guide you. Keep pursuing Jesus with all your strength. Soon you will be able to enter into his loving presence, both now and forevermore.

*For the time is coming when
people will not put up with sound doctrine,
but having itching ears, they will accumulate
for themselves teachers to suit their own desires,
and will turn away from listening to the truth
and wander away to myths.*

2 Timothy 4:3–4

CHAPTER VII

Denouncing the Sin of Idolatry
Testing the Spirits

All forms of divination are to be rejected: recourse to Satan or demons, conjuring up the dead or other practices falsely supposed to "unveil" the future. Consulting horoscopes, astrology, palm reading, interpretation of omens and lots, the phenomena of clairvoyance, and recourse to mediums all conceal a desire for power over time, history, and, in the last analysis, other human beings, as well as a wish to conciliate hidden powers. They contradict the honor, respect, and loving fear that we owe to God alone.[2]

Many years ago, before my encounter and conversion with the Lord, I found myself hungry for a deeper spiritual experience. I knew there was more to God than what I was experiencing, so one Sunday morning after Mass I went to the Tattered Cover bookstore. After entering the building, I noticed a magnificent staircase that swept through all three levels.

As I climbed the stairs toward the religion section, it felt like all the bright, shiny book covers were competing for my attention. After looking through the religious titles, I ventured into the spirituality section and came across a book on spirit guides. The premise of the book was for the reader to cry out to the spiritual realm and introduce themselves to special spiritual friends who would help them make decisions in life.

There were compelling testimonies from the people who wrote the book plus many others who had called out to spiritual friends and had great experiences. One man introduced himself to the heavenly beings, and afterward they helped him acquire a great amount of wealth. Another spirit guide helped a woman became more assertive in her relationships, and now she is happily married.

To begin this process, the book suggested that I should call upon the names of two very ancient-sounding entities. It also suggested that I should hold several crystals in my hands and sit near some live houseplants. After making all the necessary preparations, I sat down beneath a tall ficus plant in my bedroom and started chanting the names of the spirit guides.

At first nothing seemed to happen. So I tried calling harder and louder. The more I called out to the spirit guides, the more frustrated I felt myself growing toward God. I had no reason to be frustrated with the Lord, but the more I called out to the spirit guides, the more I could feel anger rising up from inside of me.

At the time, I had no idea that what I was reading was a very dangerous book on how to communicate with the demonic realm. I have been Catholic my entire life, and no one had warned me about New Age practices: *All practices of magic or sorcery, by which one attempts to tame occult powers, so as to place them at one's service and have a supernatural power over others—even if this were for the sake of restoring their health—are gravely contrary to the virtue of religion. These practices are even more to be con-*

demned when accompanied by the intention of harming someone, or when they have recourse to the intervention of demons.³

Clearly the Catholic Church condemns all such practices, but at the time, I didn't know any better. When I was sitting on the floor calling out to these so-called spiritual friends, I was actually praying to demons. I was in direct violation of the First Commandment, and through my sin of idolatry, the demons had every right to interfere with my spirituality.

I had only tried to communicate with spirit guides once, and the experience didn't last more than five minutes, but it was enough to hinder my walk with the Lord. On the surface, nothing appeared to happen, but soon after this experience, I found myself procrastinating before going to Mass.

I usually went to the eight o'clock Sunday service, but when 7:55 arrived, I found myself feeling lazy and making excuses. Ten minutes later it was too late to go, so I made plans to attend the next service. When it was time to leave for the ten o'clock Mass, the same thing happened. I stalled around making more excuses. Eventually, I was able to attend the noon service, but even then I found myself walking in late.

This behavior went on for months. Finally, I had to stop myself and dig down deep into my heart to figure out what was going on. At the time, I had no answers to explain my actions, but after seeking the Lord's forgiveness for not wanting to go to Mass, I felt myself being washed clean.

Looking back at this situation, I realize that when I was calling out to the spirit guides, the demons were trying to gain access to my soul by making me angry with God. If I had allowed myself to grow angry with God, and thereby denounce his lordship over that area of my life, then God would be forced to remove his Spirit from me. Once his Spirit departed, I would have been left unprotected and open for attack. At that point, the demons could have entered my life and started interfering with my spirituality.

The sin of idolatry is the most destructive of all sins, because it allows demons direct access to the victim's spirituality. Maybe that's why God made it the first of all the Commandments: *I am the Lord your God, who brought you out of the land of Egypt, out of the house of slavery; you shall have no other gods before me. You shall not make for yourself an idol, whether in the form of anything that is in heaven above, or that is on the earth beneath, or that is in the water under the earth. You shall not bow down to them or worship them; for I the Lord your God am a jealous God.*[4]

Most people think an idol is just a dead piece of wood, but when people commit the sin of idolatry, they are actually communicating with the demonic. Worship given to idols flows through the dead piece of wood into the spiritual entities operating behind the wood. Saint Paul makes this point clear in 1 Corinthians 10:20, when pagans were sacrificing to idols: *What pagans sacrifice, they sacrifice to demons and not to God. I do not want you to be partners with demons.*

There are only two spiritual forces at work in the world—God and the devil. Whenever anybody starts praying to spiritual entities other than the Blessed Trinity, they run the risk of violating the First Commandment and entering into a relationship with the demonic. It doesn't matter if the person realizes what they are doing or not. God has set up the spiritual laws of the universe, and once those laws are broken, the repercussions will take effect.

The spiritual laws of the universe work the same as the natural laws. It doesn't matter if a person believes in gravity or not. If a person refuses to believe in the existence of gravity and walks off a ten-story building, he will fall to the ground and experience the natural consequences of his actions. The same is true with the sin of idolatry. It doesn't matter if a person believes in the devil's existence or not. Anytime someone calls out to spiritual entities other than the Blessed Trinity, they are in danger of interacting with the demonic.

When this happens, the demons will usually appear to be helpful and friendly. If I had allowed myself to get mad at God and invited the spirit guides into my soul to help me make decisions, I'm sure they would have appeared as angels of light. The Bible says, *Satan disguises himself as an angel of light.*[5] After the spirit guides appeared to me in a helpful and friendly manner, I'm sure they would have started demanding more sacrifices, leading me into deeper forms of bondage.

WARNING I

This is one of the first warning signs that the sin of idolatry has been committed. Jesus never forces anyone to worship him. Demons on the other hand, will pester and torment their victims into deeper forms of bondage. They will constantly demand from their victims more prayers and greater commitments of suffering and sacrifices.

The sin of idolatry is a growing problem within the Church for several reasons: First of all Wicca witchcraft is reported to be the fastest growing religion among high school students. Books like the Harry Potter series are establishing a hunger in young children to obtain occult powers. On the surface it all seems like harmless fun, but when the spiritual laws of the universe are broken, the destructive consequences will take effect.

It doesn't matter if the kids believe in the devil or not. Anytime someone starts crying out for spiritual powers from any source besides the Blessed Trinity, the demons have the right to answer their prayer requests. Not only is the sin of witchcraft a growing problem all across Europe, North America, and Australia, but the sin of idolatry has also found its way inside the Catholic Church.

The Catechism defines the sin of idolatry as follows: *Idolatry not only refers to false pagan worship. It remains a constant temptation to faith. Idolatry consists in divinizing what is not God.[6] An idolater is someone who "transfers his indestructible notion of God to anything other than God."[7]*

Anytime someone violates the First Commandment and commits the sin of idolatry as defined in the Catechism, they are opening themselves up to the demonic. This is a very serious problem in the Church today, because very few people understand the proper way to pray in communion with the saints.

To start with, all prayers need to be focused on God. Prayer is defined in the Catechism as: *The elevation of the mind and heart to God in praise of his glory.*[8] *In the New Covenant, prayer is the living relationship of the children of God with their Father who is good beyond measure, with his Son Jesus Christ and with the Holy Spirit.*[9]

Notice that all prayer needs to be focused on God. According to the above definition, prayer is communion with God. We run the risk of committing the sin of idolatry when we start praying to spiritual entities other than God. A good example of this comes from the Holy Rosary. According to the tradition of the Church, the Rosary is a meditation on the life of Christ. When praying the Rosary, we should be praying in communion with Mary to God. When we give the honor and reverence that is due God alone, and focus it on spiritual entities other than God, we commit the sin of idolatry.

Once the sin of idolatry is committed, the demons will have the right to interfere with your spirituality. There's a healthy way to pray the Rosary in communion with Mary, keeping your devotion focused on Christ, and an unhealthy way to pray the Rosary, where in your heart you are not praying to God at all.

WARNING II

Another warning sign that you may be experiencing is the constant need to offer more sacrifices. Once you allow the devil into your life through the sin of idolatry, the demons will constantly plague you for more worship. They will make you feel powerful and special for praying to them. You may even find yourself being plagued by a religious-sounding chant that beckons you for more worship.

A good example of a demonic chant occurred while I was visiting Italy. On the first half of the trip, I had the most euphoric time with the Lord riding a scooter through the rolling hills of Tuscany. I was traveling the winding roads through the breathtaking countryside, visiting the magnificent monasteries that where built upon the hilltops. I could feel the loving presence of the Lord as if he were riding along with me the entire time. I was so touched and moved by how good the Lord was being to me, that I offered to spend the next day in ministry doing whatever he wanted.

The next morning I felt the Lord calling me to return the scooter and ride the bus to the outskirts of town. I didn't want to return the scooter, but because I wanted to be obedient to the Lord, I did as he asked. I took the bus to the place where I felt he wanted me to get off, and after looking around, I wondered if the Lord wanted me to go hiking. There appeared to be a wide, open space leading up a hill, so I started walking beside a dry irrigation ditch.

At one point I had to cross a fence. I didn't

know how to speak Italian, so I pulled out my phrase book and looked up the words *Lost, please help.* Eventually, I came across an elderly man working in his garden. After I repeated the words from the phrase book to him, he pointed up the hill, saying something that sounded like, *Holly Christna, Holly Christna.* I didn't know what he was saying, but it sounded like a good idea to keep moving, so after thanking him, I continued walking up the hill.

As I approached the top of the hill, I could see a large compound. Sure enough, it was a Hare Krishna temple. After reaching the top, I met a beautiful Italian girl and started talking with her. She invited me inside the temple, and we sat on the floor and talked for hours. I was very interested in learning more about her religion, and she seemed very interested in learning about the Christian faith. We spoke about everything from premarital sex, to why Jesus died on the cross for the forgiveness of her sins.

At one point in our conversation, some people came in and shut the curtain behind the glass area. I asked her what was going on, and she said, "It's time for the gods to eat." There were two statues inside the glass area, one male and the other female. The members of her community were bringing food and setting the plates before the statues. After the curtain was reopened, I could feel our conversation winding down.

When I was getting ready to leave, it felt like I was being watched. All during the conversation, I felt very comfortable sitting on the floor talking as if we were the only two people in the room; but from the other side of the room, I could feel something coming from a large statue. At first the statue looked fake, but the presence behind the statue was so strong, I started wondering if it were real. At that point I realized there was a demonic spirit behind the statue, and I wanted to get out of there as soon as possible.

As we were leaving, the young girl offered me some yogurt. There was a dish sitting by the door. I didn't want to refuse her hospitality and run the risk of offending her, because I had just spent two hours telling her about the Lord. I wanted to leave a good impression, so I accepted a spoonful of yogurt. As soon as I did, the Hare Krishna chant started playing in my head.

After I left the compound, the chant plagued my thoughts for about a week. It was so strong that I was scared it would never leave me alone. It was the same chant that the young girl said drew her into the Hindu religion in the first place. All during this time I prayed that God would open the Italian girl's eyes to the deception that she was under. I never went back to the compound or saw the girl again, but I still pray for her to this day.

This experience was a valuable lesson about the dangers that lurk behind the sin of idolatry. Once the doorway has been opened, the demons will continue chanting, harassing, and tormenting their victims until they receive more worship. In the same way, if you have committed the sin of idolatry in your religious behaviors, you may be experiencing a never-ending chant that beckons you to pray to spiritual entities other than the Blessed Trinity.

WARNING III

Another way to determine if you have been committing the sin of idolatry is to discern if you are driven to justify your beliefs by acquiring more information. For example, if you have developed an unhealthy Marian devotion, you may feel compelled to read more books on the topic to support your views. Slowly you may notice your spiritual focus shifting off of the Lord Jesus and onto the Blessed Mother.

A good example of this shift in theology comes from a church in Texas. After the pastor built a shrine to the Virgin of Guadalupe, many of the members started hearing from Mary on a regular basis. The only problem was that they were all hearing conflicting messages—all at the same time. The problem with hundreds of people hearing from Mary all at the same time is that Mary is not omnipresent.

God is the only omnipresent Deity who can be in all places at all times. When Mary appeared at Fatima, it was not possible for her to appear at Lourdes at the same time. The Holy Spirit can speak to a man in China and to a man in New York at the same time, because God's Spirit in omnipresent.

Satan, demons, humans, saints, and angels do not have the power to be in two places at the same time. Satan can assign one demon to a man in China and one demon to a man in New York, but the same demon cannot be in two places at the same time. The same is true with our guardian angels. One angel may be in heaven receiving messages, while another angel is standing guard on earth, but one angel cannot be in two places at the same time.

WARNING IV

Another way to discern if you have been committing the sin of idolatry in your religious behaviors is to test the spirits. If an apparition of Mary appears and starts giving you personal messages, then you should be able to ask the voices in your head if they bow down and serve the Lord Jesus Christ of Nazareth who came in the flesh.

According to Sacred Scripture, we should test the spirits to make sure they are coming from God and not from demons operating under religious-sounding names. *Beloved, do not believe every spirit, but test the spirits to see whether they are from God; for many false prophets have gone out into the world. By this you know the Spirit of God: every spirit that confesses that Jesus Christ has come in the flesh is from God, and every spirit that does not confess Jesus is not from God. And this is the spirit of the antichrist, of which you have heard that it is coming; and now it is already in the world.*[10]

If the voices that are bringing you messages cannot confess Jesus as their Lord and Master, then ask Jesus to send his warring angels to have the spiritual entities destroyed. If Jesus really did send his Mother to give you a special message, or if the message is coming from your guardian angel, then both Mary and your guardian angel will be able to pass the test by acknowledging the Lord Jesus Christ as their Master.

WARNING V

Another problem that has surfaced within the Church are the consecration vows to spiritual entities other than the Blessed Trinity. These vows can be dangerous because they require the person making the vow to sell their soul and the value of all their good deeds to spiritual entities other than the Blessed Trinity. These vows are dangerous because demons have the right to operate under any name and title they want.

For example, in the Book of Jeremiah demons were operating under the name Queen of Heaven. God sent his prophet Jeremiah to the exiles living in the land of Egypt to warn them by saying, *"Thus says the Lord of hosts, the God of Israel: You yourselves have seen all the disaster that I have brought on Jerusalem and on all the towns of Judah. Look at them; today they are a desolation, without an inhabitant in them, because of the wickedness that they committed, provoking me to anger, in that they went to make offerings and serve other gods that they had not known, neither they, nor you, nor your ancestors. Yet I persistently sent to you all my servants the prophets, saying, 'I beg you not to do this abominable thing that I hate!'"*[11]

Then all the men who were aware that their wives had been making offerings to other gods, and all the women who stood by, a great assembly, all the people who lived in Pathros in the land of Egypt, answered Jeremiah: "As for the word that you have spoken to us in the name of the Lord, we are not going to listen to you. Instead, we will do everything that we have vowed, make offerings to the queen of heaven and pour out libations to her."[12]

In this situation, the demons were operating under the name Queen of Heaven. God told them to stop and called their sin of idolatry an abomination, yet they continued, because the demons had been giving their victims special powers. In response to Jeremiah's warning from the Lord, they said, *"We used to have plenty of food, and prospered, and saw no misfortune. But from the time we stopped making offerings to the queen of heaven and pouring out libations to her, we have lacked everything and have perished by the sword and by famine."*[13]

And the women said, "Indeed we will go on making offerings to the queen of heaven and pouring out libations to her; do you think that we made cakes for her, marked with her image, and poured out libations to her without our husbands' being involved?"[14]

The demonic stronghold that had developed through the sin of idolatry was too great. Demons operating under the name Queen of Heaven had entered into the people's minds and hearts, and they were unwilling to denounce their false gods and turn back to the Lord. Unfortunately, the same is true today. If demons can operate under the name Queen of Heaven, they can also operate under the name Mary, Immaculata, or the Blessed Mother.

WARNING VI

Another unhealthy practice is the novena to Saint Jude. This prayer card advises Catholics that if they make eighty-one copies of the prayer and leave nine copies in the church for nine consecutive days, then God will grant them anything they ask. This type of behavior is unhealthy, because it falls under the category of superstition as defined in the Catechism: *To attribute the efficacy of prayers or of sacramental signs to their mere external performance, apart from the interior dispositions that they demand, is to fall into superstition.*[15]

The Saint Jude novena falls under the category of superstitious behavior because God is not obligated to do anything you ask just because you leave nine copies of a prayer card in church for nine consecutive days. When you commit the sin of superstition and start praying to spirit entities other than God, the religious spirits will be very motivated to answer your prayer request.

Religious spirits are always looking for ways to divert the adoration and devotion that is due to God and capture it for themselves. When the religious spirits have the power to give you what you want, they are very motivated to answer your prayer requests, knowing you will promote the devotion to all your friends. And by so doing, you will be taking the spiritual worship away from God and placing the focus on superstitious practices.

This would be another way to determine whether or not you have been committing the sin of idolatry in your religious behaviors. When you pray to God, does the Lord seem cold, distant, and far removed? But when you pray to spirit entities other than God, are your prayer petitions answered almost immediately? If so, this may be a good indicator that you are not praying to God at all.

WARNING VII

Burying a statue of Saint Joseph upside down in your backyard is another example of superstitious behavior. You can usually find these capsules for sale in almost every Catholic shop across the nation. Burying the statue in the ground is another form of superstition because if your house does sell, then all the glory goes to a piece of plastic. The capsule gets the worship, and it robs the homeowner of their responsibility for making Jesus the Lord over their business endeavors and financial affairs.

If you have been committing the sin of idolatry, taking vows of consecration, or have been involved in New Age practices, you may find yourself unable to enter into the Lord's presence. The religious spirits that you have been making agreements with will do everything in their power to keep you away from the Lord. They will demand more and more idol worship from you, driving you farther away from the truth.

If you have been committing the sin of idolatry by reading horoscopes, playing with the Ouija board, practicing dream channeling, summoning a spirit guide, visiting a hypnotherapist, participating in a séance, casting spells, practicing Wicca witchcraft, taking vows with the Mormons or Masons, or have been involved in any other occult activity, take a minute right now to denounce these vows in the name, power, and authority of Jesus. Tell the Lord that you are sorry for turning to false gods for power, insight, and the fulfillment of your prayer requests.

If you have been committing the sin of idolatry

in your religious behaviors by giving the honor and reverence that is due God alone to spiritual entities other than the Blessed Trinity, take a minute right now to repent. Turn back to the Lord with your whole heart and your full devotion. If you have sold your soul and the value of all your good deeds to spiritual entities operating under religious-sounding names, denounce those vows right now in the name of Jesus. Say the words out loud: *In the name of Jesus, I break every harmful and destructive agreement that I have made with the enemy.*

If you are a parish priest who has failed to take responsibility for the spiritual well-being of your congregation, take a minute right now to repent and ask the Lord to show you how to make amends for your actions. According to the Catechism, it is the clergy's responsibility to monitor all forms of popular piety:

Pastoral discernment is needed to sustain and support popular piety and, if necessary, to purify and correct the religious sense which underlies these devotions so that the faithful may advance in knowledge of the mystery of Christ.[16]

For the sake of your tradition,
you make void the word of God. You hypocrites!
Isaiah prophesied rightly about you when he said:
"This people honors me with their lips,
but their hearts are far from me;
in vain do they worship me,
teaching human precepts as doctrines."

Matthew 15:6–9

CHAPTER VIII

Overcoming Spiritual Stagnation
Moving with the Power

These signs will accompany those who believe: by using my name they will cast out demons; they will speak in new tongues; they will pick up snakes in their hands, and if they drink any deadly thing, it will not hurt them; they will lay their hands on the sick, and they will recover.[2]

According to Sacred Scripture, every baptized believer should be exhibiting these signs. As disciples of Christ we have been given authority over all the works of the devil. It is our responsibility to drive the presence of evil out of our lives, families, and spiritual sphere of influence. According to the Catechism, those who have accepted the sacrament of Confirmation should have received the same out-pouring of the Holy Spirit as the disciples did on the day of Pentecost.

It is evident from its celebration that the effect of the sacrament of Confirmation is the special outpouring of the Holy Spirit as once granted to the apostles on the day of Pentecost.[3]

From this fact, Confirmation brings an increase and deepening of baptismal grace:

—it unites us more firmly to Christ;

—it increases the gifts of the Holy Spirit in us;

—it gives us a special strength of the Holy Spirit to spread and defend the faith by word and action as true witnesses of Christ...[4]

Once the disciples were filled with the Holy Spirit, they went forth to heal the sick, cast out demons, and preach the Good News. They even became more resilient to sickness and disease. A good example of the ability to fight off deadly poison comes from the life of Saint Paul. He was under arrest on his way to Rome to face charges when a severe winter storm caused the ship to run aground near Malta.

Since it had begun to rain and was cold, they kindled a fire and welcomed all of us around it. Paul had gathered a bundle of brushwood and was putting it on the fire, when a viper, driven out by the heat, fastened itself on his hand.[5]

When the natives saw the creature hanging from his hand, they said to one another, "This man must be a murderer; though he has escaped from the sea, justice has not allowed him to live."[6]

He, however, shook off the creature into the fire and suffered no harm. They were expecting him to swell up or drop dead, but after they had waited a long time and saw that nothing unusual had happened to him, they changed their minds and began to say that he was a god.[7]

Saint Paul was an ordinary man; the only difference between him and the natives was the infilling of the Holy Spirit, which he received through the laying on of hands. It was the Holy Spirit's power that made his body immune to the viper's deadly venom. It's the same power that all Catholics receive at their Baptism and Confirmation—the power to heal the sick, drive out demons, and proclaim the Gospel message.

After Paul cast the deadly viper back into the fire, the chief of the island, Publius, received him into his home for three days. *It so happened that the father of Publius lay sick in bed with fever and dysentery. Paul visited him and cured him by praying and putting his hands on him. After this happened, the rest of the people on the island who had diseases also came and were cured.*[8]

In the same way, Stephen, who was *full of grace and power, did great wonders and signs among the people.*[9] Peter was anointed with so much power that the townspeople *carried out the sick into the streets, and laid them on cots and mats, in order that Peter's shadow might fall on some of them as he came by.*[10] And according to the Word of God, *they were all cured.*[11]

In the same way that these ordinary men were called by God to become disciples of Christ, so too are all Catholics called to become disciples of Christ. The same outpouring of the Holy Spirit that filled Peter the apostle, Stephen the deacon, and Paul the Jewish convert, is the same power that all Catholics receive at their Baptism and Confirmation.

The process of moving with the Lord's power starts with a full and complete surrender. After you place your life into the Lord's hands, it will be necessary to start spending time listening to the calling he has placed on your life. After the Lord gives you your first assignment, it will be necessary to follow in complete obedience. Step-by-step, the Lord will lead you into greater ministry assignments that will allow you to operate with a greater outpouring of the Holy Spirit.

If you are not able to discern the Lord's calling for your life and listen to his personal instructions, you can also begin this process by following his written instructions. All of the Lord's directives are clearly stated in Sacred Scripture; all you need to do is study the Word of God and apply his teachings to your life. A good way to begin this process would be to obey the Third Commandment.

Remember the sabbath day, and keep it holy. Six days you shall labor and do all your work. But the seventh day is a sabbath to the Lord your God; you shall not do any work—you, your son or your daughter, your male or female slave, your livestock, or the alien resident in your towns. For in six days the Lord made heaven and earth, the sea, and all that is in them, but rested the seventh day; therefore the Lord blessed the sabbath day and consecrated it.[12]

For most of us, Sunday is our only day off. Instead of honoring the sabbath, many parishioners show up at church for an hour and then spend the rest of the day shopping, doing laundry, working in the yard, paying bills, and worshiping the false god of football. Our lives get so busy with entertainment, soccer games, and household chores, that there's hardly any time left for God.

Not only is keeping the sabbath day of rest one

of God's Commandments, but it will not be possible to develop a deeper relationship with Christ without spending time with him. Most people would like to blame the problem on the lack of time, but everybody has been given the same amount of time. We have all been given twenty-four hours per day, the same amount of time Jesus had when he walked the face of the earth.

The problem is not the lack of time, but the way we choose to spend our time. Many parishioners have a desire to drive newer cars, live in bigger houses, play with better toys, and take longer vacations. To afford all the luxuries of the world, we usually overextend our finances and end up working six days a week to pay for everything. Sunday is our only day off, so we give God an hour at Mass, and spend the rest of the day playing catch-up.

If God, "rested and was refreshed" on the seventh day, man too ought to "rest" and should let others, especially the poor, "be refreshed." The sabbath brings everyday work to a halt and provides a respite. It is a day of protest against the servitude of work and the worship of money.[13]

I used to think that taking a day off from moneymaking activities was considered a day of rest. After spending a day at the beach in Mexico, I discovered the true meaning. At the time I was working on a book project and had made a long-term commitment to fast on juice and water. I would work six days a week on the book and take a day of rest on Sunday. About halfway through the project, I decided to spend my day of rest at the beach.

I had a house on the waterfront, but swimming in the aqua-blue lagoon wasn't as good as swimming in the ocean. I lived about thirty minutes away from the beach, but the water was rough and appeared to be dirty because of the large industrial port nearby. The closest white-sand beach was about an hour away. The only problem was that the road getting there was extremely rough. I didn't want to drive my truck over all the potholes, so I decided to take the bus.

The idea sounded like a great way to spend the sabbath. What could be better than a peaceful day at the beach with the Lord? I began the journey by loading some juice and water in my backpack. After attending morning Mass, I caught a bus heading out of town. The ride was slow and bumpy. The bus was old and loud. There were exhaust fumes coming from a plate on the floor near my feet. The trip took longer than I expected, but within two hours I reached my destination.

I was expecting to spend a peaceful day on the beach with the Lord, but when I arrived, the wind had picked up and the bright and beautiful sunny morning had turned into a cloudy, cold afternoon. After walking around a while, I grew tired and wanted to go home. The fast had made me physically weak. I didn't have the energy and enthusiasm that I would normally have for a day at the beach.

I had to wait about an hour for the next bus to arrive, and once again, it took two hours for the return trip. Upon my arrival, I was exhausted. I wanted to spend the sabbath's day of rest with the Lord getting refreshed and recharged so that I could have a productive workweek, but with all the physical activity, I nearly killed myself.

If I hadn't been fasting, I'm sure the day at the beach would have been great, but because of my weakened state, I learned a very important lesson—the purpose of the sabbath rest is exactly that, to rest and be refreshed. It is supposed to be a day to commune with the Lord.

The very next Sunday I spent the entire day at rest. After attending morning Mass, I went back home and spent the remainder of the day with the Lord. I asked God to give me some Scripture passages that I needed to read. I allowed the Word of God to minister to my spirit. I made my favorite juice and spent the day sitting on the boat dock dangling my feet in the water. After taking a candlelight bath in the evening, I felt perfectly rested and refreshed. My spirit was recharged, and I was able to start my workweek with a profound new perspective.

I realize the process of keeping the sabbath rest may seem like an additional burden, given all the stress and pressure that the average parishioner may be experiencing, but that is exactly why God gave us the command. If you take one day a week and totally dedicate yourself to the Lord, it will be like taking fifty-two, spirit-filled retreats every year. Not only will your relationship with the Lord begin to grow, but you will also receive the necessary grace to conduct a more productive workweek.

Another way that I was able to break away from

all the worldly attachments of materialism so that I could serve the Lord more fully was to start tithing. I learned the power of tithing after purchasing my first rental property. At the time, I was only nineteen years old. I had just closed a deal on a bright red house located near a noisy highway. It was my intention to rent out the top half of the house and build an apartment in the basement.

Right after closing, I went to work building a wall that sealed off the back door from the kitchen. I placed a rental ad in the paper, and within a short period of time, I found a family who wanted to move into the top unit. During this time, I continued to work on the basement apartment. Everything was going great until the day I knocked on the front door to collect my tenant's rent. When I asked for the money, the lady who answered the door said, "Because you are making so much noise in the basement, we're not going to pay you."

I was shocked. I needed their money to make my first mortgage payment. Not knowing what to say, I blurted out, "If you don't pay me, I'm going to evict you."

"Go ahead and evict us. It will take you six months to get us out of here!"

I stood on the front porch for a brief moment shocked and speechless, and then the lady slammed the door in my face. I was devastated. I had spent all my savings buying materials to work on the basement. I only had $287 to my name, and I needed $713 to make my first mortgage payment.

I didn't have any friends who would loan me $500. I was too ashamed to ask my parents for help, because they didn't want me buying the property in the first place. With nowhere else to turn, I surrendered the situation to the Lord and threw all my money in the church collection basket. My situation seemed so hopeless—why not give God a try?

After I gave all my money to God, things took a turn for the worse. My tenants called me later that afternoon and said, "You had better get down here right away! Your clothes dryer burned up all our laundry. Firemen broke down the front door. We are going to sue you for damages."

I arrived right as the fire truck was pulling away. My harvest-yellow clothes dryer was sitting in the front yard. Only now it was harvest yellow and black, because of all the burn marks across the front. When I walked inside the house, my tenants were packing their belongings into boxes. "What's going on now?" I asked.

"We're moving," they said.

The smoke damage inside the house was unbearable. All the doors and windows were open, but after being inside for only a brief moment, the terrible stench of burned plastic started making my eyes burn.

By the next day the tenants had completely vacated the property. I called my insurance company to see if they could reimburse me for the loss. After the adjuster calculated the costs to wash the walls and fix the front door, he said, "How does $2,800 sound?"

I was overjoyed and gratefully accepted his offer. About an hour later, another man knocked on the door and said, "Hi, my name is Don. I'm a public insurance adjuster. Can I talk with you about your claim?"

"You're too late. I just settled about an hour ago."

"Do you mind if I look at the figures?" Don said. "A lot of times I can help the insured get a better settlement."

"Sure," I said, handing him the paperwork.

"You settled too cheap," Don said. "They paid you to *wash* the walls. They should have paid you to *repaint* all the walls. If you want, I can get you a better settlement."

After looking over his contract, I realized there was nothing to lose. Don was only charging a ten percent commission on the additional funds that he collected, so I signed his agreement, and within a short period of time, he had acquired an additional $2,000.

Once again, I was overjoyed. After I had placed all my money into the church collection basket, God had successfully evicted the tenants and put $4,800 in my pocket. I was able to make my first mortgage payment and still had plenty of money left over.

After experiencing the miracle-working power of God, I started taking tithing a lot more seriously. I started giving ten percent of my income on all my business endeavors. The more I gave to God, the more he gave back to me. Soon I discovered the promise described in Malachi 3:8–10.

Will anyone rob God? Yet you are robbing me! But you say, "How are we robbing you?" In your tithes and offerings! You are cursed with a curse, for you are robbing me—the whole nation of you! Bring the full tithe into the storehouse, so that there may be food in my house, and thus put me to the test, says the Lord of hosts; see if I will not open the windows of heaven for you and pour down for you an overflowing blessing.

After experiencing the power of this promise, I quickly realized that by giving to the Lord, I grew closer to him in several ways. First of all it helped me to learn obedience. As a disciple of Christ, it is my responsibility to advance God's kingdom here on earth. It's not possible to advance God's kingdom when my life is consumed with greed, materialism, and the pursuit of money. Tithing helped me break the bondage of materialism and set my eternal perspective in the proper order.

Giving is an important part of any relationship. If I'm always taking from the Lord and never giving, it may lead to an attitude of selfishness, which has the ability to hinder my relationship with him. When I give to the Lord, it helps deepen my love. When I give out of love and obedience, God is more empowered to open up the windows of heaven and pour upon me an overflowing blessing.

Tithing is also an important element in becoming a disciple of Christ. If you can't give God a small percentage of your income, then the same sin of selfishness may also be preventing you from laying down your life in complete surrender and obedience. By spending time with the Lord, keeping the sabbath rest, and breaking the bondage of materialism, God will be more empowered to start working with you on the greater calling that has been placed on your life.

The process of becoming a disciple of Christ starts with your obedience to Christ. By spending time communing with the Lord on your day of rest, you will be more empowered to hear his softly spoken voice and discern your calling. For example, if during your quiet time the Lord gives you a vision for a healing ministry, then all you need to do is start small by praying with your friends and family members.

If God is calling you to minister to the elderly, then start by visiting a nursing home. If God is calling you to minister to the homeless, consider spending a weekend on the streets, or better yet, take a homeless man out to lunch. Step-by-step, the Lord will meet you in your ministry efforts. It is only when we step out in faith, in obedience to the calling that he has placed on our lives, that God supports us with his miracle-working power.

Take a minute right now to examine your heart. Have you been honoring the sabbath by allowing yourself to spend a full day of rest being refreshed and recharged in the Lord's presence? If you are a priest or lay minister who needs to work on Sunday, are you keeping a day of rest on your next available day off? Are you spending time with the Lord getting recharged so that you have something to share with your congregation the rest of the week?

All ministry flows from our relationship with the Lord. Without spending the necessary time in the Lord's presence, it's very easy to burn out and end up spiritually depleted with nothing to give. If you are guilty of spiritual burnout, make a commitment to start honoring the sabbath on your first available day off.

If you have been putting worldly activities and the love of sporting events before the Lord, make amends for your actions. Make a commitment right now to put your relationship with Christ as the first priority in your heart. If you have found yourself ensnared by the ways of the world, ask the Lord to set you free. Ask Jesus to show you anything clsc in your life that's hindering your relationship with him. Ask him to remove all false gods from your life, so that you can serve him more fully.

If you are guilty of throwing your leftover change into the church collection basket, take a minute to ask the Lord's forgiveness. The Lord deserves your full love and devotion. If you have been withholding what belongs to God, make a commitment to start giving your best to him. Bring the full tithe into his storehouse and then ask him to open the windows of heaven and pour upon you an overflowing blessing.

If you have been neglecting the gifts of the Holy Spirit, take a moment to ask your heavenly Father's forgiveness. Ask the Holy Spirit to come into your life and bring the gifts of wisdom, faith, healing, prophecy, discernment of spirits, the gift of tongues, and the ability to perform miraculous signs. In doing so you will be more empowered to exhibit the Lord's miracle-working power.

Strive to enter through the narrow door; for many,
I tell you, will try to enter and will not be able.
When once the owner of the house
has got up and shut the door,
and you begin to stand outside
and to knock at the door,
saying, "Lord, open to us,"
then in reply he will say to you,
"I do not know where you come from."

Luke 13:24–25

CHAPTER IX

Undefiled Works of Religion
Inviting Christ into Your Heart

Not everyone who says to me, "Lord, Lord," will enter the kingdom of heaven, but only the one who does the will of my Father in heaven. On that day many will say to me, "Lord, Lord, did we not prophesy in your name, and cast out demons in your name, and do many deeds of power in your name?" Then I will declare to them, "I never knew you; go away from me, you evildoers."[2]

Picture yourself standing before God's throne on the day of judgment. The fullness of the Lord's divinity is radiating from his presence like dazzling white light. As the books are being opened, Jesus turns to a vast crowd of people who were expecting to enter their heavenly rest and says to them, "I never knew you; go away from me, you evildoers."

One man questioned the Lord, "What do you mean? We know who you are. I have a crucifix and a miraculous medal inscribed with your image."

Jesus says a second time, "I'm sorry, but I never knew you."

"What about all my good deeds? I spoke to other people about you and performed many works of power in your name. What do you mean, *I never knew you?*"

Then Jesus turns to the man and says, "You did a lot of good works in my name, all that is true. You also practiced a lifetime of religious behaviors, but you never established an intimate relationship with me. You never allowed my lordship into your life. You never listened to my voice. You never followed my guidance. You never accomplished the will of my Father in heaven."

"I was doing everything everybody else was doing," the man said.

"The will of my Father was never accomplished in your life, because you never established an authentic relationship with me. My Father had specific plans for you. He created you for a purpose and wanted specific responsibilities carried out that were never fulfilled. You never even bothered to ask me, not once. I stood at the door of your heart, knocking every day of your life, but you were too busy practicing the works of religion."

"What about the rest of these people?" the man said.

"Have you never read the Scripture passage where it says, *'Enter through the narrow gate; for the gate is wide and the road is easy that leads to destruction, and there are many who take it. For the gate is narrow and the road is hard that leads to life, and there are few who find it.'*"[3]

My deepest concerns are for my fellow brothers and sisters who are traveling the wide and easy road of religion. It takes almost no effort to show up at Mass for an hour on Sunday and say a few Hail

Marys throughout the day. Even those who are working in full-time ministry performing many deeds of power in the Lord's name, run the risk of hearing the Lord say, "I never knew you."

Do you know the risen Lord Jesus Christ? Have you surrendered your life into his service? Do you spend time in prayer listening to his softly spoken voice? Are you following the Lord in complete obedience? There's a difference between practicing religious behaviors and actually being connected to the life-giving source.

Jesus says, *"I am the true vine, and my Father is the vinegrower. He removes every branch in me that bears no fruit. Every branch that bears fruit he prunes to make it bear more fruit. You have already been cleansed by the word that I have spoken to you. Abide in me as I abide in you. Just as the branch cannot bear fruit by itself unless it abides in the vine, neither can you unless you abide in me."[4]*

"I am the vine, you are the branches. Those who abide in me and I in them bear much fruit, because apart from me you can do nothing. Whoever does not abide in me is thrown away like a branch and withers; such branches are gathered, thrown into the fire, and burned."[5]

In the same way that branches are connected to the vine, so too are all Catholics required to maintain an intimate connection with Jesus. Branches with a solid connection to the vine are able to produce good fruit. Branches that have been cut off from the vine cannot produce anything. Without an intimate connection to Jesus these branches wither and die.

Without an intimate, life-giving connection to Jesus, it is not possible to produce any kind of spiritual fruit. Anyone can perform good deeds, but there's a difference between doing good works and accomplishing the will of the Father. For example, let's say I decide to start performing good deeds like washing people's windows.

If I took a bucket of water and a sponge to the nearest shopping mall, I could approach a parked car and start washing the windshield. When the owner of the car saw what I was doing, he would probably come running over screaming, "Get away from my car!" I may try to explain my good intentions, but he would probably kick my bucket of water over and drive away angry.

At the end of the day, I may feel pretty good about myself. In my prayer time, I may say things like, "Look at what a good person I am! Aren't you proud of me, God? Today, I washed more than fifty windshields. I would have stayed longer, except the security guard starting persecuting me."

When God looks at this situation, he would probably consider it all a waste of time. If I took the time to develop an authentic relationship with the Lord, learned how to listen to his voice, and spent the necessary time practicing contemplative prayer, I may hear the Lord say something like, "I never asked you to go to the mall and wash windows. Nothing you did produced any eternal value. You caused damage to my name. Many were offended, and no one experienced any kind of spiritual conversion."

Now imagine that after spending an hour communing with the Lord, I felt called to visit the mall. I may not know why the Lord is calling me to the mall, but out of obedience, I obey his command. Upon arriving I may see a young man sitting on the sidewalk wearing a black T-shirt and ripped jeans.

When I'm connected to the life-giving vine, I should be able to ask the Lord, "What do you want me to do here?" If the young man keeps coming to my thoughts, I could ask the Lord, "Do you want me to talk with him?" I may have no idea what to say, but when I'm connected to the life-giving vine, the love of God will flow through me.

Jesus knows exactly what is going on in this young man's life. He knows that the boy has run away from home and has spent the night outside in the cold. Jesus knows his pain. Jesus knows the exact words that need to be spoken to cut through the young man's defensiveness and penetrate his heart.

It is only when I'm obedient to the Lord, fully surrendered in his service, and connected to the life-giving vine that I can produce good fruit that will last. When I allow myself to be filled with God's love, I can approach the young man with compassion. If I allow Jesus to speak his words through me, I will be able to move past the young man's defensive exterior.

The Lord may want me to buy him breakfast. The Lord may want me to spend the afternoon with him just hanging out. The Lord may want me to share with him how he can have his sins forgiven and be filled with the Holy Spirit. The Lord may want me to help reconcile the differences and reunite the boy with his parents. It is only through a life-giving relationship with Jesus that any kind of eternal fruit can be produced.

Another example of our need to be connected to the Lord's life-giving source comes from the story of the ten bridesmaids. In the Gospel of Matthew, Jesus tells a story about those who failed to make the necessary preparations by keeping their lamps burning brightly. *Five of them were foolish, and five were wise. When the foolish took their lamps, they took no oil with them; but the wise took flasks of oil with their lamps.[6]*

As the bridegroom was delayed, all of them became drowsy and slept. But at midnight there was a shout, "Look! Here is the bridegroom! Come out to meet him." Then all those bridesmaids got up and trimmed their lamps. The foolish said to the wise, "Give us some of your oil, for our lamps are going out." But the wise replied, "No! there will not be enough for you and for us; you had better go to the dealers and buy some for yourselves."[7]

And while they went to buy it, the bridegroom came, and those who were ready went with him into the wedding banquet; and the door was shut. Later the other bridesmaids came also, saying, "Lord, lord, open to us." But he replied, "Truly I tell you, I do not know you." Keep awake therefore, for you know neither the day nor the hour.[8]

The bridesmaids were not allowed into the

heavenly banquet, because they failed to keep the light of Christ burning brightly in their ministry efforts. They failed to make the necessary preparations. They lived a lifetime without ever taking their calling seriously. They were called to be light in a world of darkness. The Lord wanted his light to shine through their lamps and into the lives of others. Because they didn't make the necessary preparations, their lamps went out. Afterward the Lord sealed the door shut and said, *"I do not know you."*

In another parable, the Lord summoned his slaves and entrusted his property to them; *to one he gave five talents, to another two, to another one, to each according to his ability. The one who had received the five talents went off at once and traded with them, and made five more talents. In the same way, the one who had the two talents made two more talents. But the one who had received the one talent went off and dug a hole in the ground and hid his master's money.*[9]

After a long time the master of those slaves came back to settle accounts with them. The man who used his talents wisely was greatly rewarded for his service. He was able to enter into his master's joy. But the man who buried his talents came forward and said, *"Master, I knew that you were a harsh man, reaping where you did not sow, and gathering where you did not scatter seed; so I was afraid, and I went and hid your talent in the ground. Here you have what is yours."*[10]

But his master replied, "You wicked and lazy slave! You knew, did you, that I reap where I did not sow, and gather where I did not scatter? Then you ought to have invested my money with the bankers, and on my return I would have received what was my own with interest. So take the talent from him, and give it to the one with the ten talents. As for this worthless slave, throw him into the outer darkness, where there will be weeping and gnashing of teeth."[11]

In the same way, every baptized believer has been entrusted with talents, each according to his or her own ability. On the last day, the book of life will be opened and everybody will need to render an account. Those who have wasted their talents out of fear, laziness, or worldliness, run the risk of being cast into the outer darkness. Those who have accomplished the Father's will for their lives, will be greatly rewarded.

The process of using your talents wisely can begin in one of two ways. One way is to develop an authentic relationship with Jesus. Once you learn how to listen to the Good Shepherd's voice, he will start giving you personal assignments that he wants you to accomplish. After you set out to accomplish the Father's will for your life, the Lord will start working with you, giving you the necessary strength and grace to accomplish what he has asked.

Step-by-step, your relationship with the Lord will grow. After you complete one assignment, you will need to seek the Lord to receive your next assignment. By maintaining a connection to his life-giving source, you will receive the necessary nourishment to produce everlasting fruit. Step-by-step, your relationship with the Lord will grow, leading you into deeper levels of intimacy, allowing you to accomplish greater works for the kingdom of heaven.

The other way is to start doing good works without developing an authentic relationship with Jesus. If you are unable to hear the Good Shepherd's voice, you can start the process by being obedient to the Word of God. Because the Bible commands all Christians to make disciples of all nations, all you need to do is go forth and start ministering to the lost, hurting, and the needy. Once you attempt to produce good works, you will quickly realize your inability and complete dependence on Christ.

After you acknowledge your need to receive life-giving nourishment from the vine, simply cry out to the Lord for help. Invite the Spirit of Jesus to come into your heart to give you the necessary strength. Start spending time with the Lord to receive nourishment from his life-giving source. Step-by-step, your relationship will begin to grow, and soon you will be producing fruit that will endure to everlasting life.

Take a minute right now to evaluate your eternal destination. On the last day, will you be able to look the Lord in the eyes, knowing that you have accomplished everything that he has asked you to do? Are you actively listening to the voice of the Good Shepherd and faithfully producing fruit for the kingdom of heaven? Are your religious behaviors leading you into a deeper relationship and dependence on Christ? Has there ever been a time when you surrendered your life to the Lord and invited his Spirit to dwell inside of your heart?

One of the most profound encounters I have ever experienced with the Lord occurred the day I received a vision of my heart. I was sitting on the floor praying when the power of the Holy Spirit over-shadowed me. I could feel the supernatural grandeur and majesty of God all around.

When the Lord showed me my heart, it was small, cold, and insignificant. It looked like it was made out of metal and had a tiny door that opened and closed. In that moment of truth, I realized that I had never invited the divine presence of God to dwell inside of my heart.

God's grandeur was so bright and brilliant, like a vast ocean of pure love, truth, and warmth. It was too much for me to endure. After a brief moment, the vision grew too intense, and I had to break away. Soon I found myself back in my bedroom sitting on the floor.

I took the calling from God very seriously. I got back in prayer and re-created the vision from my memory. I pictured the metal heart and imagined a tiny door opening as I prayed the words; *I invite you into my heart. Please send your Holy Spirit to dwell inside of me.* Nothing happened, so I tried opening the door wider and praying harder, but nothing changed. I didn't feel any different. I knew the vision was from God and that it was true. I was withholding my heart because I was scared. Deep down inside of me, I was reluctant to give God the most sacred part of my being.

After thinking about the vision, I realized I was scared to give God my heart, because I have been hurt many times in the past. Whenever I gave my heart to a woman, it usually turned out disasterous.

I have fallen in love several times, and after I opened up my heart to these women, they had the ability to cause me a lot of pain.

Falling in love is the richest and most passionate experience I have ever encountered, but unfortunately the breakups can be devastating. Not only did my girlfriends have the ability to hurt me after I had fallen in love with them, but they could also take advantage of my vulnerability.

After thinking about this further, I realized I was projecting my human-relationship dynamics upon the Deity. I was scared to invite the Spirit of the Lord into the most sacred parts of my being, because every time I had given my heart to a woman, I ended up getting hurt.

After thinking about the vast beauty and magnificence of God's grandeur in comparison to my emptiness, I was forced to make a decision. Would I live my life with a cold heart, or would I invite the richness, beauty, and splendor of the Lord to dwell inside of me.

Eventually, I made a decision for Christ. I centered myself deep in prayer and recalled the vision of the tiny heart. I spoke the words from the core of my being. *Dear Jesus, please do anything you want with my life. I surrender everything into your hands. Come into my heart and create in me the kind of person you have intended me to be.*

After my prayer time, I didn't feel any different. The vast ocean of God's great love didn't fill me to overflowing, and soon I began to worry. I called a spiritual friend to pray with me. She invited me over to her house, and after I shared the vision with her, we decided to go to the mountains and pray some more.

We drove about thirty minutes, and after parking the car, we walked up a dirt road toward the top of the mountain. The sun was about to set for the evening, and the sky was illuminated in a thousand different shades of yellow and orange.

After we arrived at the top, we sat on a rock outcrop and watched the sparkling city lights below. With the unspoken words of my inner being, I invited the presence of the Lord to come inside. In the same way a man falls in love with a woman, I opened up my heart and fell in love with Jesus. I surrendered the core of my being to him. I made myself vulnerable to him in every way, as I gave him my everything.

Immediately, I could feel his euphoric strength enter my being. It was just like Jesus had promised when he said, *"Those who love me will keep my word, and my Father will love them, and we will come to them and make our home with them."*[12]

The divine presence of Christ had finally filled my heart, and the next day, I was on a spiritual high. I could actually feel the Lord's presence inside of me. Whenever I started to pray, a great wellspring would rise up inside of me.

Before my encounter with the Lord, it would take me several hours of prayer to reach the deep levels that I now experience after just a few short minutes. Before the mountaintop experience, it felt like God was somewhere up in the clouds, distant, and far away—like my prayers to God would hit the top of my head and stop.

Now when I pray, the presence of the Lord is right here inside of me. His presence dwells inside of my soul. I don't need to shoot prayer arrows into the clouds anymore. I can commune with the Lord anytime I want. I have the testimony of the Son of God living inside of me, just like it's described in Sacred Scripture: *Those who believe in the Son of God have the testimony in their hearts. Whoever has the Son has life; whoever does not have the Son of God does not have life.*[13]

After my mountaintop experience, even the words *I love you, Jesus,* took on a whole new meaning. Before they didn't mean much, because I had never met Jesus. I knew who he was, but I never had a real live encounter with the risen Lord until the day I invited his Spirit into my heart. After meeting Jesus, I could feel my love for him welling up inside of me every time I said the words, *I love you, Jesus.*

Was there ever a time when you opened up your heart in complete surrender to the Lord? Have you ever fallen deeply in love with Jesus and invited his Spirit to dwell inside of you?

You may want to take some time right now to pray. Find a quiet place in your home, or on a mountaintop. Dig down deep inside your heart and offer the Lord's Spirit an invitation to come inside of your soul. Fall in love with Jesus the same way you would fall in love with a romantic lover.

The God of the universe desperately desires to create a passionate love affair with you. Plunge deep into the vast ocean of his life-giving love and allow the sacred romance to begin.

Whenever you pray,
do not be like the hypocrites;
for they love to stand and pray in the synagogues
and at the street corners, so that
they may be seen by others.
Truly I tell you, they have received their reward.
But whenever you pray,
go into your room and shut the door
and pray to your Father who is in secret;
and your Father who sees in secret
will reward you.

Matthew 6:5–6

156

CHAPTER X

Catholic Revival Prayers

The Prayer of Saint Francis

O great and glorious God, enlighten the darkness of my mind. Grant me enduring faith, certain hope, and perfect charity. Help me to embrace the depths of your love, that in all my ways, I may accomplish your good and perfect will.

Consecration to the Holy Spirit[2]

On my knees before the great multitude of heavenly witnesses, I offer my whole self, mind, body, heart, and soul to you, Eternal Spirit of God. I adore the brightness of your purity, the unerring keenness of your justice, and the might of your love.

You are the strength and light of my salvation. I desire to never grieve you by my unfaithfulness, and I pray with all my heart to be kept from the smallest sin against you. Mercifully guard my every thought and grant that I may always watch for your guidance, listen to your voice, and follow your holy inspirations.

I cling to you, give myself to you, and ask by the grace of your compassion that you watch over me in my weakness. Holding the pierced feet of Jesus and looking at his five wounds, trusting in his precious blood, and adoring his opened side and stricken heart, I implore you, adorable Spirit, helper of my infirmity, to keep me in your grace that I may never sin against you. Amen.

Prayer of Surrender

Dear Lord Jesus, it is my will to surrender to you everything that I am and everything that I'm striving to be. I open the deepest recesses of my heart to you and invite your Holy Spirit to dwell inside of me. You are the salvation of my soul; I hold nothing back from you.

I offer you my mind, heart, body, soul, spirit, emotions, all my hopes, plans, and dreams. I surrender to you my past, present, and future problems, habits, character defects, attitudes, livelihood, resources, finances, occupation, skills, vocation, and business endeavors. I surrender everything unto your compassionate care.

I give you my home, marriage, sexuality, relationships, friendships, and children. I surrender all my weaknesses, strengths, fears, and insecurities to you. In sickness and in health, in the good times and bad, I belong to you. Please transform my life into whatever most pleases you. Transform me into the child of God that you have intended me to be.

Psalm 119[3]

Teach me, O Lord, the way of your statutes, and I will observe it to the end. Give me understanding, that I may keep your law and observe it with my whole heart. Lead me in the path of your commandments, for I delight in it. Turn my heart to your decrees, and not to selfish gain. Turn my eyes from looking at vanities; give me life in your ways.

When I think of your ordinances from of old, I take comfort, O Lord. Your statutes have been my songs wherever I make my home. I remember your name in the night, O Lord, and keep your law. At midnight I rise to praise you, because of your righteous ordinances. Teach me good judgment and knowledge, for I believe in your commandments.

Before I was humbled I went astray, but now I keep your word. It is good for me that I was humbled, so that I might learn your statutes. Your hands have made and fashioned me; give me understanding that I may learn your commandments. Let your mercy come to me, that I may live; for your law is my delight. I will never forget your precepts, for by them you have given me life. Oh, how I love your law! It is my meditation all day long.

Your word is a lamp to my feet and a light to my path. Accept my offerings of praise, O Lord, and teach me your ordinances. I rise before dawn and cry for help; I put my hope in your words. My eyes are awake before each watch of the night, that I may meditate on your promise. In your steadfast love hear my voice; O Lord, in your justice preserve my life.

Denouncing Religious Spirits

Heavenly Father, in the name of your Son, my Lord and Savior, Jesus Christ, I denounce the sin of idolatry, superstitious practices, and all vows of consecration that I have made to spiritual entities other than the one true God—the Blessed Trinity. I denounce the practice of offering prayers and worship to false gods and selling my soul along with the value of my good deeds to spiritual entities operating under religious-sounding names.

I denounce all forms of divination, seeking oracles from the dead, communicating with mediums, spirit guides, all practices of the New Age movement, Zen Buddhism, Reiki, astrology, horoscopes, fortune-telling, palm readings, magic charms, and anything associated with the occult or Satan. I denounce all of these practices in the name of the Lord Jesus Christ who came in the flesh, and by the power of his cross, his blood, and his resurrection, I break their hold over me.

O most Sacred Heart of Jesus, fountain of every blessing, I confess all these sins before you and ask you to cleanse and forgive me. I adore you, love you, and need you. O good and loving Jesus, grant that I may always live in you, through you, and for you. Send forth your Holy Spirit and baptize me with power from on high, just as you baptized your disciples on the day of Pentecost.

Infilling of the Holy Spirit[4]

O most Holy Spirit, I acknowledge that I can do nothing of eternal value without your assistance. Come then, O most Holy Spirit, and fulfill the promise of my blessed Savior when he said, *"I will not leave you orphaned."* Come into my heart. Descend upon me as on the day of Pentecost when you filled your first disciples with power from on high. Grant that I may fully participate in all your gifts that you bestow with such great generosity.

Take from my heart whatever is not pleasing to you and make of it a worthy dwelling place for your holy presence. Illuminate my mind that I may see and understand the things that are for my eternal good. Inflame my heart with pure love that I may be cleansed from the impurity of worldly attachments. Strengthen my will that I may conform to your divine will and be guided by your holy inspirations. Aid me by your grace to practice the divine lessons of humility, poverty, obedience, and contempt for all worldly ways, which Jesus taught through his mortal way of life.

O rend the heavens and come down, consoling Spirit! So that inspired and encouraged by your power, I may faithfully fulfill the duties of my calling and endeavor to accomplish your divine will with the utmost perfection. Spirit of love! Spirit of purity! Spirit of joy! Sanctify my soul more and more and give me that heavenly peace that the world cannot give. May your will be done in me and through me, that your holy presence may be praised and glorified forevermore.

Prayer for Reconciliation

Almighty and merciful Father, I implore your forgiveness for all the times I have sinned against your holy Catholic Church. Please forgive me for disrespecting anything that was sacred, for spreading gossip, being angry, criticizing the priest's homily, and projecting negative word curses. Please send forth your Holy Spirit to repair and restore all the damage that I have caused in the past.

Merciful Lord Jesus, I ask for your grace to forgive all members of the clergy who have ever hurt me. I forgive my parish priest for all his harmful actions and unkind words that he has spoken against me. I forgive all those in positions of authority, especially any members of the clergy who have violated my mental, emotional, and spiritual well-being. I ask for your loving grace to heal all the circumstances where I failed to receive the love and support that I needed from my parish community.

By an act of my free will, I choose to forgive everybody, including the people who hurt me the most. I release my desire to receive an apology, my need to be justified in my actions, and my need for others to acknowledge the injustice. I surrender the entire debt of all injuries into your merciful hands, Lord Jesus. I denounce all forms of anger, bitterness, and resentment, and I command any evil spirits that have attached themselves to me through the lack of forgiveness to leave now and go straight to the feet of the Lord, Jesus Christ.

Through the power of your Holy Spirit, I ask you, Lord Jesus, to fill me with your love, joy, peace, kindness, generosity, and self-control. May your healing hand rest upon me now as I bless all those who have hurt me. I desire to be kind and compassionate to everyone, forgiving them just as you have forgiven me. Amen.

Prayer for a Spiritual Canopy

Almighty and merciful Father, I come before you to intercede on behalf of your holy Catholic Church. I beseech thee, Lord, to send forth your purifying fire to cleanse every aspect of my parish community. I ask that you establish an impenetrable spiritual canopy around the congregation where I worship. Please wash and purify everything inside this spiritual canopy with your most precious blood, Lord Jesus Christ.

I ask you to send forth your angelic army to strike down and destroy all forms of demonic spirits that have come against your holy Catholic Church. Destroy and bind to the abyss all demons and their devices that have access to my parish through the sins of idolatry and superstitious behaviors. Send forth your warring angels to strike down and destroy all anti-Christ spirits, religious spirits, and any other demonic spirits of perversion, stagnation, and complacency.

Drive out all demonic spirits of division and isolation that have been preventing your Holy Spirit's bond of brotherly love. Send forth your power to create in our community a desire for authentic Christian fellowship. Help us to establish the loving bonds of a healthy, caring community. Drive out all demonic spirits of oppression and heaviness that are militating against your Holy Spirit's gift of joy-filled celebration, sanctification, and freedom in Christ.

I ask you to destroy all demonic spirits of fear, shame, self-condemnation, false forms of guilt, unhealthy desires to suffer, and all other forms of unworthiness. Send forth your Holy Spirit to lead the entire congregation into your heavenly courts to experience your loving presence. Flood the minds and hearts of everyone who enters through the doors of our parish community with an authentic spirit of praise, as we bow down and worship your magnificent presence.

Prayer to the Divine Consoler[5]

O Divine Consoler, I adore you as my true God, with God the Father and the Son. I adore you and unite myself to the adoration you receive from all your angels and saints. I give you my heart and offer you my endless praise for all the grace that you never cease to bestow upon me.

O giver of all supernatural gifts, I beg you to visit me with your grace and grant me the gift of holy fear, so that it may prevent me from falling back into my past sins, for which I beg pardon. Grant me the gift of piety, so that I may serve you with increased fervor, follow your holy inspirations with more promptness, and observe your divine precepts with greater fidelity.

Grant me the gift of knowledge, so that enlightened by your holy teaching, I may walk the path of eternal salvation without deviation. Grant me the gift of fortitude, so that I may courageously overcome all the assaults of the devil that threaten the salvation of my soul. Grant me the gift of counsel, so that I may choose what is more conducive to my spiritual advancement.

Grant me the gift of understanding so that I may comprehend the divine mysteries, and by contemplation of heavenly things, may detach my thoughts and affections from the vain things of this material world. Grant me the gift of wisdom, so that I may rightly direct my actions, referring them to God as my ultimate destiny; so that after loving and serving him in this life, I may experience the happiness of possessing him for all eternity.

Prayer for the Spirit's Conviction

Dear Lord Jesus, I ask you to send forth the power of the Holy Spirit into the lives of everyone in my parish community. If any members of the clergy are ensnared with the sins of clericalism, legalism, hypocrisy, spiritual pride, complacency, teaching false doctrines, exhibiting pharisaical attitudes, or displaying an outward form of godliness while inwardly denying your power, I ask you to send forth the gift of your Holy Spirit's conviction.

If any members of the laity are polluting the spiritual atmosphere of the Church through their sins of idol worship, clergy worship, superstitious behaviors, complacency, spiritual stagnation, legalism, materialism, gossip, judgmental or pharisaical attitudes, I ask you to send forth the power of your Holy Spirit to convict them of their sins. Gently lead all sinners back into a state of grace where they can authentically connect and commune with you in spirit and in truth.

Please purify the spiritual atmosphere and airspace that surrounds your sacred assembly. Cleanse the congregation so that your Holy Spirit may dwell inside the lives and hearts of all your beloved children. May the grandeur of your holy presence be so profoundly encountered within your courts that all your children will ignite with a fervent passion to serve you all the days of their lives. I ask this through my Lord Jesus Christ, your Son, who lives and reigns with you and the Holy Spirit, one God, forever and ever. Amen.

Consecration to the Sacred Heart

Precious Lord Jesus, I consecrate my entire life and every fiber of my being unto your divine will, service, and glory. Transform all that I am and all that I'm striving to be into your perfect image and likeness. Unite the love that burns deep within my heart to the passionate love that burns within your most Sacred Heart.

Precious Lord Jesus, you are the guardian of my soul, the assurance of my salvation, the remedy for my weakness, the atoning sacrifice for my sins, and my only refuge at the hour of my death. Be then, O most Sacred Heart of Jesus, my justification before God the Father.

I put all my hope, confidence, and trust in you. Remove from me all that is displeasing to you and all that resists your holy will for my life. May the purity of your love impart your presence so deeply within my heart that I may never be separated from you. Amen.

Prayer to Purify the Church

Spirit of our God, Father, Son, and Holy Spirit, most Holy Trinity, descend upon your holy Catholic Church. Purify and cleanse the magisterium, priesthood, sanctuary, worship space, sacristy, religious objects, icons, statues, parish office buildings, community space, schools, and retreat facilities. Banish all the forces of evil from the Church's property and presence.

If any occult members have infiltrated our parish community or are praying curses against the congregation, I ask you to strip them of their psychic powers, demonic powers, and occult powers. Please strip them of all magic charms, veils, psychic vision, and powers of divination. Please have all their powers and devices destroyed and cast into the abyss.

By the power of your command, I ask you to destroy all curses, hexes, voodoo practices, satanic rituals, incantations, and all evil assignments that have been sent against your sacred assembly. Destroy all spells, witchcraft, black magic, diabolic infestations, oppressions, possessions—all that is evil and sinful—gossip, idolatry, apathy, complacency; and all psychological, moral, and spiritual ailments.

By the power of the Lord God Almighty, in the name of Jesus Christ my Savior, I command all the evil influences that have infiltrated my worship space to leave now and to be consigned into the everlasting lake of fire, that they may never again harm me or any other creature in the entire world.

Prayer to Sanctify the Priesthood

Almighty Father, please send forth the power of your Holy Spirit upon the priesthood. May your life-changing grace transform the minds and hearts of all your disobedient and unfaithful priests into your own image and likeness. Stir in them the grace of their vocation. Keep them close to you at all times, lest the enemy prevail against the sanctity of their souls.

May the passion of your Spirit's power ignite the hearts of your beloved preachers. May your servants' hands burn with your anointed power as they minister to those who are sick and in need of your healing touch. May their sermons captivate the congregation with your prophetic words as they reprove, teach, and encourage the flock. May they be filled with the fire of your love, so that their lives and ministries reveal your true presence in the world. May they flow with the same miracle-working power that your disciples exhibited on the day of Pentecost.

O merciful Father, may your Spirit's power accompany your servants everywhere the soles of their feet tread. Protect them from the wicked snares of the devil that are continually being set against the just. Expose the evil deeds of those with hardened hearts, so that they may be brought to repentance. Remove any unhealthy priests that need to be removed from your service. Place a canopy of protection around all your faithful priests and bestow upon them every spiritual blessing in the heavenly places.

Prayer for the Indwelling[6]

Holy Spirit, powerful Consoler, sacred bond of the Father and the Son, hope of the afflicted, descend into my heart and establish in me your loving domain. Enkindle in my tepid soul the fire of your love, so that I may be wholly subject to you.

O Holy Spirit, when you dwell within our hearts you also prepare a dwelling place for the Father and the Son. Come then, O great Consoler of abandoned souls and protector of the needy. Help the afflicted, strengthen the weak, and support the wavering. Come and purify me. Let no evil desire take possession of me. You love the humble and resist the proud. Come to me, glory of the living and hope of the dying. Lead me by your grace that I may always be pleasing to you.

Litany for the Saints Militant[7]

For the Holy Father, *flood him with your grace, Lord*. For all Cardinals, Archbishops, and Bishops, *fill them with the gifts of your Holy Spirit*. For all diocesan priests, *strengthen them in their work, Lord*. For all priests who are ill, *heal them, Lord*. For all priests in danger, *deliver them with your mighty hand, Lord*. For all priests who are weak, *sustain them, Lord*. For all priests who are being tempted, *may they be kept holy in body and soul*.

For all priests who want to know you more deeply, *enkindle their hearts with the passion of your Holy Spirit*. For all priests who are depressed, *console them, Lord*. For all priests who are worried, *give them your peace, Lord*. For all priests who are elderly, *strengthen them, Lord*. For all priests who are alone, *keep them in your company, Lord*. For all priests who direct souls, *grant them your wisdom, Lord*. For all priests who are under spiritual attack, *may they be transformed into mighty men of valor, Lord*.

For all holy men and women of God, *grant them your life-changing grace, Lord*. For all those who serve your Church, *fill them with your loving virtues, Lord*. For all those who work in the mission field, *give them a burning desire to save souls, Lord*. For all those who minister to the poor, *grant them patience, charity, and generosity, Lord*. For all those who work in the parish office, *give them obedience and kindness, Lord*. For all those who comfort the grieving, *give them the gifts of counsel and compassion, Lord*. For those who minister to the lost, homeless, hurting, and imprisoned, *give them strength in their labors, Lord. Amen.*

Prayer for Seminarians

Almighty God and everlasting Father, I implore your blessing upon all those attending seminary. Grant the abundant outpouring of your wisdom to all those placed in the authority of instructors and teachers. May your seminarians grow in grace day by day, as you enlighten their minds, subdue their wills, and purify their hearts.

May all your theological students grow deeper in love, humility, and holiness, as they experience your divine presence more profoundly within their hearts. Help these men keep themselves mentally alert, physically fit, and spiritually pure, and by your constant presence in their work, rest, and play, enable them to grow into the virtues that characterize a holy priesthood.

Prayer for Vocations

O gracious and loving Father, according to your word, the harvest is plentiful but the laborers are few. Send forth then, O most Holy Spirit, a calling to all the holy men and women of our community. Grant them the discernment to hear your softly spoken voice and the courage to answer your call. Give them the wisdom to realize the precious gift of consecrated life.

Shine forth your heavenly light upon the paths that you have chosen for all your beloved children. Open the doors that need to be opened and close the doors of worldly allurements and distractions that need to be closed. Fill their hearts with a burning desire to please you. Bless them with the necessary grace to pursue the callings that you have placed upon their lives.

A Prayer for Priests[8]

Keep them, O Lord, for they are thine, your priests whose lives burn brightly before your blessed shrine. Keep them, for they are in the world, though from a world apart; when earthly pleasures tempt and allure, shelter them in your most Sacred Heart.

Keep them and comfort them in hours of loneliness and pain, when all their lives of sacrifice for souls seem but in vain. Keep them and shelter them, O Lord, as they have no one but thee, for they have tender hearts of human frailty. Keep them as spotless as thy Host, that daily their hands caress; their every thought, word, and deed, dearest Lord, I ask for you to bless.

Spiritual Affirmation Scriptures

The following scripture passages have the power to draw you into a deeper relationship with the Blessed Trinity. According to the Catechism, *God is the author of Sacred Scripture. The Sacred Scriptures contain the Word of God and, because they are inspired, they are truly the Word of God.*[9]

By meditating on God's Word, your mind will be renewed and your identity as a child of the King will be restored. When you find yourself struggling with difficulties, try repeating the verse from Philippians 4:13 over and over again. *I can do all things through him who strengthens me.*

Soon you will be able to move with the same power that Christ promised to all believers when he said, *"Amen, amen, I say to you, whoever believes in me will do the works that I do, and will do greater ones than these, because I am going to the Father. And whatever you ask in my name, I will do, so that the Father may be glorified in the Son."*[10]

Genesis 1:27 & 31	Matthew 28:18–20
Isaiah 62:3–5	Mark 16:15–18
Jeremiah 31:31–34	Luke 10:1–2
Joel 2:28–29	Luke 10:17–20
Matthew 3:11	Luke 11:9–13
Matthew 10:1	Luke 15:11–24

John 1:12	1 Corinthians 14:1–4
John 7:37–39	2 Corinthians 5:20
John 10:27–28	2 Corinthians 10:3–5
John 14:8–23	Ephesians 1:3–6
John 15:4	Ephesians 2:19–22
John 17:20–23	Ephesians 3:11–12
Acts 1:8	Ephesians 3:16–19
Acts 2:38–39	Philippians 1:6
Acts 5:32	Philippians 4:4–7
Romans 8:10–11	Colossians 1:11–14
Romans 8:14–17	Colossians 3:12–17
Romans 8:28	2 Timothy 1:6–7
Romans 8:31–39	Hebrews 4:16
1 Corinthians 3:16	Hebrews 12:1
1 Corinthians 6:19–20	James 1:27
1 Corinthians 12:7–11	1 John 5:10–12

Notes

I. Since the Dawn of Creation—The Deadly Assault
1. Gustave Doré, a detail of "Nailing Christ to the Cross,"
   The Bible Gallery (New York: Cassell & Company, 1880).
2. Revelation 12:7–9.
3. Genesis 4:3–5.
4. Genesis 4:7.
5. Genesis 4:8.
6. Exodus 20:2–5.
7. Exodus 32:1.
8. Deuteronomy 18:9–12.
9. Joshua 9:15.
10. 2 Chronicles 36:14–16.
11. John 8:44.
12. Matthew 23:13–15.
13. Mark 12:28.
14. Mark 12:29–31.
15. Mark 12:32–33.
16. Mark 12:34.
17. Mark 3:2–6.
18. 2 Peter 2:1–3.

II. Call No One on Earth Your Father—Restoring Our Image of God
1. Gustave Doré, a detail of "Jesus with the Doctors,"
   The Bible Gallery (New York: Cassell & Company, 1880).
2. Matthew 23:5–9.
3. Matthew 23:9–12.
4. Catechism of the Catholic Church: 1548; Pius XII, encyclical, *Mediator Dei*: AAS, 39 (1947) 548.
5. Catechism of the Catholic Church: 783; cf. John Paul II, *RH* 18–21.
6. Catechism of the Catholic Church: 873; *AA* 2.
7. Catechism of the Catholic Church: 871; CIC, can. 204 § 1; cf. *LG* 31.
8. Catechism of the Catholic Church: 1256; CIC, can. 861 § 2.
9. Catechism of the Catholic Church: 1263; cf. Council of Florence (1439): DS 1316.
10. Matthew 28:18–20.
11. 1 Corinthians 12:12, 14 & 17.

12. 1 Corinthians 12:18–21.
13. 1 Corinthians 12:22–25 & 27.
14. Catechism of the Catholic Church: 882; *LG* 22; cf. *CD* 2, 9.
15. 2 Corinthians 5:17–20.
16. John 14:8–10.
17. John 17:21–23.

III. The Growing Trend of Suffering—Taking Authority over Evil

1. Gustave Doré, a detail of "Jesus Healing the Sick," *The Bible Gallery* (New York: Cassell & Company, 1880).
2. Matthew 12:22 & 24.
3. Matthew 12:34–36.
4. Luke 13:11–13.
5. Luke 13:15–16.
6. Catechism of the Catholic Church: 105; *DV* 11.
7. Catechism of the Catholic Church: 215.
8. Catechism of the Catholic Church: 135; *DV* 24.
9. Job 2:7.
10. 2 Timothy 1:7 New American Bible.
11. Catechism of the Catholic Church: 2852; St. Ambrose, *De Sacr.* 5, 4, 30: PL 16, 454; cf. *Rom* 8:31.
12. Catechism of the Catholic Church: 520; *GS* 38; cf. *Rom* 15:5; *Phil* 2:5.
13. Luke 9:1–2.
14. Luke 10:17–19.
15. Daniel 10:12–13.
16. 2 Timothy 1:8.
17. 1 Peter 3:16–17.
18. Acts 16:16–18.

IV. Communion with Christ—Establishing an Authentic Relationship

1. Gustave Doré, a detail of "The Last Supper," *The Bible Gallery* (New York: Cassell & Company 1880).
2. 1 Corinthians 11:27–30.
3. Catholic Answers, Tom Meagher, *Don't Bequeath Catholic Ignorance to Your Children* (San Diego: Catholic Answers, 1999).
4. Catechism of the Catholic Church: 1324; *LG* 11.
5. Catechism of the Catholic Church: 1324; *PO* 5.
6. Oregon Catholic Press, *Breaking Bread with Daily Mass Propers 2007* (Portland: Oregon Catholic Press, 2006), p. 17.

7. Oregon Catholic Press, *Breaking Bread*, p. 22.
8. Oregon Catholic Press, *Breaking Bread*, p. 22.
9. Oregon Catholic Press, *Breaking Bread*, p. 22.
10. Oregon Catholic Press, *Breaking Bread*, p. 25.
11. Matthew 5:24.
12. 1 Corinthians 11:27.

V. Surrender Your Life to the Lord—Following in Complete Obedience

1. Gustave Doré, a detail of "Jesus at the House of Martha and Mary," *The Bible Gallery* (New York: Cassell & Company, 1880).
2. Catechism of the Catholic Church: 260; cf. *Jn* 17:21–23; *Jn* 14:23.
3. Matthew 25:31–33.
4. Matthew 25:34–36.
5. Matthew 25:37 & 40.
6. Matthew 25:41–43.
7. John 10:7–10.
8. John 10:11–15.
9. John 10:27.
10. Catechism of the Catholic Church: 2716.
11. Catechism of the Catholic Church: 2709; *Song* 1:7; cf. 3:1–4.
12. Catechism of the Catholic Church: 2717; cf. St. Isaac of Nineveh, *Tract.* myst. 66; St. John of the Cross, *Maxims and Counsels*, 53 in *The Collected Works of St. John of the Cross*, tr. K. Kavanaugh, OCD, and O. Rodriguez, OCD (Washington DC: Institute of Carmelite Studies, 1979), 678.
13. Matthew 25:40.
14. Luke 6:46–49.

VI. Removing the Devil's Devices—Entering into the Lord's Presence

1. Gustave Doré, a detail of "The Temptation of Jesus," *The Bible Gallery* (New York: Cassell & Company, 1880).
2. Genesis 3:1–3.
3. 1 Peter 2:13.
4. Romans 13:1.
5. Matthew 6:14–15.
6. Matthew 6:24.
7. Catechism of the Catholic Church: 2114; Origen, *Contra Celsum* 2, 40: PG 11, 861.

VII.   Denouncing the Sin of Idolatry—Testing the Spirits
1. Gustave Doré, a detail of "St. Paul at Ephesus," *The Bible Gallery* (New York: Cassell & Company, 1880).
2. Catechism of the Catholic Church: 2116; cf. *Deut* 18:10; *Jer* 29:8.
3. Catechism of the Catholic Church: 2117.
4. Exodus 20:2–5.
5. 2 Corinthians 11:14.
6. Catechism of the Catholic Church: 2113.
7. Catechism of the Catholic Church: 2114; Origen, *Contra Celsum* 2, 40: PG 11, 861.
8. Catechism of the Catholic Church: Second Edition, Glossary PG 894.
9. Catechism of the Catholic Church: 2565.
10. 1 John 4:1–3.
11. Jeremiah 44:2–4.
12. Jeremiah 44:15–17.
13. Jeremiah 44:17–18.
14. Jeremiah 44:19.
15. Catechism of the Catholic Church: 2111; cf. *Mt* 23:16–22.
16. Catechism of the Catholic Church: 1676; cf. John Paul II, CT 54.

VIII. Overcoming Spiritual Stagnation—Moving with the Power
1. Gustave Doré, a detail of "St. Peter and St. John at the Beautiful Gate," *The Bible Gallery* (New York: Cassell & Company, 1880).
2. Mark 16:17–18.
3. Catechism of the Catholic Church: 1302.
4. Catechism of the Catholic Church: 1303; cf. Council of Florence (1439): DS 1319; *LG* 11; 12.
5. Acts 28:2–3.
6. Acts 28:4.
7. Acts 28:5–6.
8. Acts 28:8–9.
9. Acts 6:8.
10. Acts 5:15.
11. Acts 5:16.
12. Exodus 20:8–11.
13. Catechism of the Catholic Church: 2172; *Ex* 31:17; cf. 23:12; cf. *Neh* 13:15–22; 2 *Chr* 36:21.

IX. Undefiled Works of Religion—Inviting Christ into Your Heart

1. Gustave Doré, a detail of "The Last Judgment," *The Bible Gallery* (New York: Cassell & Company, 1880).
2. Matthew 7:21–23.
3. Matthew 7:13–14.
4. John 15:1–4.
5. John 15:5–6.
6. Matthew 25:2–4.
7. Matthew 25:5–9.
8. Matthew 25:10–13.
9. Matthew 25:15 & 16–18.
10. Matthew 25:24–25.
11. Matthew 25:26–28 & 30.
12. John 14:23.
13. 1 John 5:10 & 12.

X. Catholic Revival Prayers

1. Gustave Doré, a detail of "Jesus Praying in the Garden," *The Bible Gallery* (New York: Cassell & Company, 1880).
2. Holy Spirit Fathers.
3. Psalm 119:33–37, 52, 54, 55, 62, 66, 67, 71, 73, 77, 93, 97, 105, 108, 147–149.
4. Unknown author.
5. Saint Alphonsus Liguori.
6. Saint Augustine of Hippo.
7. Unknown author.
8. Unknown author.
9. Catechism of the Catholic Church: 105 & 135; *DV* 11; *DV* 24.
10. John 14:12–13 New American Bible.

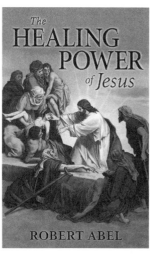

If you would like to participate in our ministry, please consider spreading the message from the *Roman Catholic Revival*. To purchase additional copies of this book for ministry purposes, or to make a donation, please use the following information:

Number of Copies	Ministry Price
3	$25
6	$40
9	$60

These prices include tax and free shipping within the United States. For shipments to other countries, please contact us. Thank you for your generous donations.

Mail your payment to:

Valentine Publishing House
Roman Catholic Revival
P.O. Box 27422
Denver, Colorado 80227